AF610551

Order this book online at www.trafford.com/08-0222
or email orders@trafford.com

Most Trafford titles are also available at major online book retailers.

Note for Librarians: A cataloguing record for this book is available from Library and Archives Canada at www.collectionscanada.ca/amicus/index-e.html

ISBN: 978-1-4251-7162-9

We at Trafford believe that it is the responsibility of us all, as both individuals and corporations, to make choices that are environmentally and socially sound. You, in turn, are supporting this responsible conduct each time you purchase a Trafford book, or make use of our publishing services. To find out how you are helping, please visit www.trafford.com/responsiblepublishing.html

Our mission is to efficiently provide the world's finest, most comprehensive book publishing service, enabling every author to experience success. To find out how to publish your book, your way, and have it available worldwide, visit us online at www.trafford.com/10510

www.trafford.com

North America & international
toll-free: 1 888 232 4444 (USA & Canada)
phone: 250 383 6864 • fax: 250 383 6804 • email: info@trafford.com

The United Kingdom & Europe
phone: +44 (0)1865 722 113 • local rate: 0845 230 9601
facsimile: +44 (0)1865 722 868 • email: info.uk@trafford.com

10 9 8 7 6 5 4 3 2

The

Catholic Talmud

Volume One
"The Nine Orders of Divinity"

Book of Instructions
In the
Christian Faith

BY

Dr. John Paul Hozvicka D.D.
Apostolic Bishop of Jesus Christ
Teacher of the Holy Scriptures
Author

The Knowledge of the Holy Scriptures is Fulfillment

Special Thanks

I thank God for helping me and guiding my thoughts in the writing of this book.

Dedication

This Biblical Commentary called the "Christian Talmud," a book of instruction in the Christian faith is dedicated to all Christian denominations of the entire world and to all that practice God's love. I dedicate this book to my brother in Christ Pope John Paul II whom I have come to respect and love as a great servant of God.

I also dedicate this book to the United States of America who has protected its citizen rights of free religion and the freedom to write and express one's opinions and thoughts.

Declaration

This personal statement is made to all Biblical students, declaring that all-religious book, manuals, magazines and pamphlets are not always free of human error and its doctrinal or moral teachings may not always be correct. It is not implied that those who have been granted permission to have their work published has the full agreement of their superiors, publishers, or church leader with regards to the content, opinions, or statements expressed. But that the freedom to think and express one's thoughts and ideals are still permitted among all the major religions of the world.

Biography

+ Dr. John Paul Hozvicka began his theological studies when he signed up and completed 18 Bible study courses from various Christian Churches throughout the United States. His hunger for Biblical knowledge could not be satisfied, so he enrolled in various Seminaries, colleges programs, and institutions Biblical study courses, earning his degrees.

+ Bachelor of Theology, St. Anthony's Seminary Nov. 5, 1989

+ Diploma, Institute of Jewish-Christian Studies
Nov. 1, 1991

+ Ordained as a Priest of "The Old Catholic Church" (an independent Church, not under the Pope of Rome) "Certificate of Ordination" Jan. 26th 1991.

+ Consecrated as Bishop, of the Old Catholic Church, "Certificate of Consecration" July 14 1991.

+ Upon his consecration as Bishop of the Old Catholic Church he was honored and awarded an honorary "Doctor of Divinity" degree from Agape Seminary, Sept. 6, 1991

+ Continuing his education he completed the required study courses and earned his Master of Divinity, Agape Seminary, 2001

Round table Discussion

To stimulate intellectual interest and to promote biblical research in the understanding of the teaching of Christianity among the various churches in the community, Dr. Hozvicka held round table discussion among the priests, elders, and ministers of the local Christine Churches in his community.

He would encourage debates and argument on the various church doctrines that separates the Christian communities everywhere.

For him this became a great learning experience. At times he would also enjoy breaking bread with his Jewish friends, especially on Passover, for Easter and Passover always fell on the same week and he respected both traditions. For Jesus was Jewish, and he observed the Jewish traditions of Passover.

Personal Achievements

* 20 years of teaching the Holy Scriptures through private tutoring and too interested groups.

* Author of "A Primer on Biblical Studies"

* Presently working on his second volume of "The Christian Talmud" entitled "The Anointed" a Bible commentary.

* Completing his third book "A Biblical Study of the Pentateuch."

Preface

I John Paul a servant and follower of Christ Jesus, by the grace of God, give unto my brothers and sisters of the world this book hereby called *"The Catholic Talmud."* I confess that the Holy Spirit has moved me and set my foot upon the path of knowledge, and gave to me the deep understanding of the spiritual things of God. I believe that it was the Holy Spirit that inspired by thoughts and guided my words.

There has always been a fascination about exploring the unknown. Man's curiosity has always motivated him to explore, seek out, and try to understand the many secrets of nature, the mysteries of God, and the purpose of his existence. Because of this, men have sought to uncover the mysteries of life and of God. They search the ocean floors, they explore the depth and recesses of caves, they fight the elements of nature, and they search the darkest jungles, and explore the rim of the universe, in search of understanding of their origin. All to quench there thirst for knowledge, and satisfied their curiosity "to know."

Within all of us there is stirring a need and desire to know the other side of reality, the spiritual things of God. *The Catholic Talmud,* is taking the first step in increasing your knowledge of the Bible and of the spiritual things of God. Through this book you have an invitation to study and learn the Holy Scriptures. In your endeavor to study the Holy Scriptures, I ask you to relax and clear your mind of the cares of this world, and let the Holy Spirit guide you through the understanding of *The Nine Orders of Divinity.*

For the word *Christian,* is a word that was developed from the word Christ, and it mean anointed and the word *Talmud,* which comes from the Hebrew language, mean "To study" or "To instruct." So we now have a clear understanding of the title of this book, an anointed book written for all Christians, to study and to find instruction in the divine things of God. During your time of study, allow the Holy Spirit to guide you. You will become aware of your inner spiritual nature. As you study, turn your thoughts upon God and his divine teachings. Open your heart and mind completely, as divine enlightenment unfolds before you.

In order to receive spiritual enlightenment, which so many people seek, and seldom achieve, you must practice daily devotion to holy prayer, then devote yourself to the practice of daily study of the Holy Scriptures. This will require much love and hard work. Don't just read the Bible, but read each word slowly, study the meaning of each word, then put everything together and receive the spiritual understanding (teaching) that the Holy Spirit will empress upon you.

My love and blessing be upon you always, In Jesus name I Pray. Amen

Dr. John Paul Hozvicka D.D.
Bishop
Brook Park, Ohio
April 29, 2007

Table of Content

Study Prayer

Dear Heavenly Father, please guide my thoughts and actions in my everyday life.

Send the Holy Spirit to enlighten me on the teachings of the Holy Scriptures.

Help me to clearly understand each chapter to its fullest understanding.

Give me the strength to read and study the Holy Scriptures, but also to faithfully practice the teachings I have learned.

I ask this in the name of Our Lord Jesus Christ. Amen.

General Articles

By

Dr. John Paul Hozvicka D.D.
Apostolic Bishop of Jesus Christ
Teacher of the Holy Scriptures
Author

I have decided to add these short articles into this book because they do relate to the purpose of this book and the subject matter. Please read these articles first before you start your study of the Catholic Talmud. They will impress upon you the importance of Scriptural study.

Article One: Personal Theology

Brothers and Sisters, I would like to open this subject on one single truth that has become the foundation of all Christian faith, "Salvation." The only thing required for salvation is two folds. 1. You're acceptance of Jesus Christ as your personal Saviour (Acts 16:31, John 3:17, 10:9, Acts 2:21 and 15:11). 2. To be baptized into Christ death in the name of the Father, and of the Son, and of the Holy Spirit (Matt. 28:19; Acts 22:16; Romans 6:3). <u>All other doctrine beyond the accepted ecclesiastical teaching of the church that is required for faith is commentary and opinions and is not required for salvation.</u>

Now that we have a clear understanding of what is required to obtain salvation, which is the single most important truth. All other theological teachings fall under the category of personal theology.

Sanctification:
A transformation of your inner nature

After you accept Christ as your personal Saviour and become baptized in the name of the Trinity, you must go through a slow process of change, a transformation of character. You will become Christ-like in nature (spiritually) *"Therefore if any man be in Christ, he is a new creature: old things are passed away; behold, all things are become new."* II Cor 5:17. You will begin to live your life according to Christ teachings and to God's will. You should no longer use profane language, smoke, drink, or take drugs, control your anger, be honest in all your dealings and no long steal or lie. Your nature will become humble, gentle, respectful, and understanding *"But the fruit of the Spirit is love, joy, peace, longsuffering, gentleness, goodness, faith, meekness, temperance: against such there is no law."* Gal. 5:22 You will yearn to study the Holy Scriptures, go to church, practice daily prayers, and participate in Church ministry and humane activities.

You're Personal Theology:

Every person reads the Holy Scriptures through their own lens, from their own perspective. Every Bible Student must read and study the Holy Scriptures through their eyes of faith.

Therefore, each person must establish his or her own personal belief, teachings, doctrine, and theology. We may run into other people who believe in what we believe in, but not always hundred percent. However, their will always is some difference; and this difference has nothing to do with salvation. Warning: Stay away from those people, preachers, minister, and friends who are not main stream in Christian teaching but practice religious fanaticism.

As each person studies the Holy Scriptures, the Holy Spirit will open their eyes according to their readiness of mind (Acts 17:11) and their inner ability to perceive and understand the truth that is being revealed. What God has revealed to you will become your personal theology. The truth that is revealed to you may not be understood by other people or maybe it will; but remember that it has become apart of your understanding and your personal theology. Everyone's personal theology and understanding is different from those of other people theology and understanding.

No two theology is always a hundred percent the same (except the oneness of the Godhead), but all that is truly important is what I have explain above in reference to salvation. Study the Holy Scriptures; and allow yourself to be open to the guidance of the Holy Spirit. When you are spiritually ready you will understand the truth that is being revealed just for you. This will be your personal theology. Hold to this theology until the Holy Spirit will reveal another idea, concept, or truth that can be added, enhanced, improve, or restructure your original personal theology. However, not all truths are totally absolute, but maybe continually unfolding to reveal a more deeply and greater truth. The guidance of the Holy Spirit may come to you directly through prayer and/or meditation or from an appointed mentor/teacher and the Church.

At times we may receive half-truths because we were not hundred percent open to receive the whole truth. In times like this we need to remain open minded until the other half is revealed. Which may take minutes, days, even years? It depends how often you study, pray, and search for the truth. I will give you an example of what had happen to me.

Example: During one of my prayer and study session I was revealed an understanding about the state of the dead. What happens when we die? What does the Bible teach about death? The truth that was revealed to me set up a number of principles by which I understood about death. This was fifteen years ago, and now I have come to realize that it was only a half-truth. I attended a funeral service and there was this minister that delivered a great sermon on what happens at the monument of death, and my mind was open to this new truth and it altered the principle of my person theology that it made me re-think my position and belief. It improved and deepened my understanding, and I saw my personal theology in a new clearer light.

Theological Indifferences

Someday this may happen to you and it does not mean your original principle was wrong, but that your truth unfolded into a newer and deeper understanding. All of theology works this way and is continually unfolding and elevating our conscious understanding. So when you discuss theology with someone who does not understand, believe or accept your theological understanding on the subject, it does not mean you or they are wrong, but are just not perceiving the same truth on the same spiritual level of understanding. Remember the Bible recognizes contradiction.

They were correct according to their readiness of mind, and their level of spiritual understanding. You are right according to your readiness of mind, to your level of spiritual understanding. The day will come when both of you will see the same truth in the same light, just give it time. So don't fight or argue over who is right and who is wrong. In a Christian round table discussion, each person explains his or her understanding of the subject that is being discussed. Each person should be open minded to each others explanation and let the Holy Spirit do the rest, and walk away from the discussion table as true Christian brothers and sisters, more spiritually enriched than before. Therefore, you have just taken part in a spiritual growth process that you were not aware of.

Blinded to the Truth

Many times people are blinded to the truth through misguided loyalty, brainwashed by false ministers and held captive through fear. These people lack the ability and courage to have an open mind to engage them selves in the search for the real truth.

For example: I recorded a sermon from a well-known minister from a Sunday morning religious show on television which he was defending God against the evolutionist. He said that God created man, and that man did not evolve from apes. I showed this program to several fundamentalists Christians who were visiting my home. They themselves were Christians, but because the minister who gave the Sermon was not from their Church, they talked against him. I could not believe what I was hearing. This minister was defending God; however, their loyalty to the Church to which they belonged lost sight of the truth and immerged themselves in religious indifference, instead of searching for truth and understanding. Even to the point of being blinded to the truth, that "God created man," they would speak against this Christian minister who was defending the faith. These people are the one's who are not open-minded and will not step a foot into another church. However, fear, ignorance, false loyalty to false minister will not watch other religious programs or listen to other sermons from other neither minister, nor read books by other good Christian authors.

I have read very good theological books that were written by various theologians from various different Christian churches in my search of understanding the truth. I have met people who would not read these theological books because they were published by other churches, and not from their church. Every Christian church has their basic belief and teaching of what they believe in or profess what they think to be the truth according to their understanding. Some of these churches teach their member to become closed minded thinkers, pretending to search for the truth, but control their members through fear and ignorance, and teach them not to trust the teachings and writings of other churches and people. All churches are in competition to keep you as their member, so your donation remains with them. A priest or ministers greatest fear is the lost of a church member who leaves the parish and joins another church.

I believe in individual personal theology. A personal theology between you and God and your conscious is answerable to no one but God. I believe in being open minded in my search for the understanding of spiritual truth. My salvation is personal between God and myself. My spiritual growth is founded on my understanding according to my personal theology. It's so important to study under the guidance of Holy Church. The Ecclesiastical "Magisterium" of Holy Church protects the truth and faith of Christ, free of error.

Article Two:
Show Thyself Approved

Brothers and Sisters, In reference to the study of the Holy Scriptures, each student of the Bible must develop his or her own personal theology, of those things that they accept and believe in that will establishes their faith. All people must show them selves approved before the eyes of God *"Study to shew thy self approved unto God, a workman that needeth not to be ashamed, rightly dividing the word of truth."* II Timothy 2:15

We must show our selves in the eyes of God to be a serious student in search of the truth, because to God, this is very important. The word "to show" comes from the Greek *"paristemi"* translated "to present" our worthiness before God in being obedient to the word found in the Holy Scriptures. We must show ourselves approved, a worker in the web of life, a master of God's divine truth. In our effort to find the truth, live it, and teach it, we must never be ashamed of what we believe in that makes up our personal theology as long as it is Biblically based.

How important is it to rightly interpret the divine truth that God has revealed in the Holy Scriptures? I once herd this minister say to his Bible student that it was not important to know the truth about everything. This same minister would accept certain words from the scriptures that he was comfortable with, and close his eyes and ears to other parts of the Bible that he did not feel was important. Was he a minister searching for the truth? I don't think so. God said we must rightly divide the word of truth. How can a true Bible student develop his or her personal theology if they don't rightly interpret the scriptures?

We must guard ourselves against the oppositions of those that would bring confusion to our understanding. Each person will slowly, over time, develop his or her personal theology of what they believe in. We do not pick and chose from the Holy Scriptures, all inspired words of God are *"…are profitable for doctrine, for reproof, for correction, for instruction in righteousness."* II Timothy 3:16

Correct understanding and knowledge of the Holy Scriptures is important and this understanding comes from keeping God's precepts *" I understand more than the ancients, because I keep thy precepts."* PS. 119:100 it has become our duty to study and practice sound doctrine *"But speak thou the things which become sound doctrine."* Titus 2:1 each student must find a mentor/teacher to study with and be guided by the Holy Spirit into sound doctrine.

God warns us about false doctrine in the Holy Scriptures that we all need to take to heart *"That we henceforth be no more children, tossed to and fro, and carried about with every wind of doctrine."* Eph. 4:14. We are to develop a hard foundation in the truth, so that every person who comes alone with a new teaching does not move us to a new false concept. We are to guard ourselves against those who do not teach God's divine truth, but teach the doctrine of men *"But in vain they do worship me, teaching for doctrine the commandments of men"* Matt. 15:9.

However, most people, after studying the scriptures for a short time, begin to think and believe that they know everything. When they reach this level in their studies they close their eyes and ears to God's warning. They're full of self-pride and inflated egos. They are no different then the Pharisee in the time of Christ, blinded to the warning.

You may now ask, how do I know when someone is teaching me the truth? Is there a method by which I can test the doctrine peoples may teach me? *"Prove all things; hold fast that which is good."* I Thess. 5:21 The Holy Scriptures is the test of all doctrines. What ever is not in harmony with the Bible is not to be accepted into your personal theology. *"Holding fast the faithful word as he hath been taught, that he may be able by sound doctrine both to exhort and to convince the gainsayers."* Titus 1:9

God has given you the gift of creative thought guided by common sense, which was developed during your younger years when you were a child. We know to take something without asking is wrong, common sense tells us this. So if someone says it's ok to take it and that person has no right to give it to you, because he is not the legal owner, then common sense says "Do not take it." Yet, so many times we allow our selves to be persuaded to ignore our inner feels and common sense. Allow God, through His Bible; show you the truth, and how to test the teachings of men.

Let your Light so shine

Once you have studied the truth and are practicing it, the Bible instructs us to let our inner spiritual light shine forth before men so others may see your good works. Thy will then come to you for counseling and understand *"Let your light so shine before men, that they may see your good works, and glorify your Father, which is in heaven."* Matthew 5:16 we are to witness the truth to others so that in their understanding of the power that works through you, they will glorify God. However, in our attempt to witness for God, we are also to guard ourselves from egotistic boasting. By boasting and bragging of our blessing and other good things we defeat the purpose of why we changed our lives and are following God teaching. We shame God and rob from him His rightly due glory.

God's whole purpose of living a righteous life is to teach us how to elevate ourselves above and beyond our self "EGO." For our ego brings us to pride which many times leads us to sin. Our ego brings us to desires of lust which leads us to sin; our ego leads us to many of the human emotions of hunger for things, envy, hate, self-pride and glory, jealousy, and many more that may lead us to sin. To live a righteous life combined with understanding, will help us to over come all of our ego misfortunes.

When you and your friends study the Holy Scriptures, allow the Scriptures to interpret themselves, and be open to the teaching of the Scriptures. You remember what the prophet Isaiah wrote *"For precept must be upon precept, precept upon precept; line upon line, line upon line; here a little, and there a little."* Isa. 28:10 In other words, God instructs us to compare scripture passage upon or against other scripture passage, verse upon verse Greek word in one passage with the same Greek word in another passage in order to understand its true meaning. This way, when we allow Scripture to interpret itself, there is very little room for error.

Article Three
The Eternal Message

Brothers and Sisters, As we read and study the Holy Scriptures we can't help but notice the repeated message that God is revealing to us. It's the same divine message of love since the fall of man when Adam and Eve were cast out of the Garden of Eden. The eternal message was then given to Abraham because of the covenant Abraham made with God, and this covenant fell upon Abraham descendents later known as Hebrews. Because Abraham made a covenant with God, his descendents became the chosen people. Through the lineage of Jesus, by way of baptism, the Christians Church then also became part of God chosen people. This opened the door for the gentiles of the Greek and Romans world that they to may become part of God's chosen people. Finally it was given to those people who practice the faith of Islam, through the teaching of the prophet Mohammed. For we are all of one family of people, all chosen children of God.

How does one become a part of the family of God and one of his chosen people? In ancient times and of all the people of the known earth, only the Hebrews, the direct descendent of Abraham chose to make a covenant with the one Most High God (Elohim) and became obedient to his laws and to his words of wisdom. Israel as a nation was no different than any other known nation. The people of Israel cheated, lied, stole, and even murdered; yet they were God chosen people. It was because they accepted God and made a covenant to be obedient. It was first put into words by Moses who first define for us who God is, *"Hear O Israel the Lord our God is one Lord"* (Deut. 6:4). God also had his message written on two tablets of stone, "I am the Lord your God there is no other gods before me." Ex. 20: 2

This truth was then passed on and accepted by the Christian Church *"Hear O Israel the Lord our God is one Lord"* (Mark 12:29). But it was advanced in theology by Jesus Christ *"baptizing them in the name of the Father, and of the Son, and of the Holy Ghost"* (Matt. 28:19). He taught One God but made of three beings, one in nature and substance, one in truth and mind *"I and my Father are one"* (John 10:30). In the name of The Father, and of the Son, and of the Holy Spirit, three personage one God. It's like one person having three different types of personality, yet still one person.

Then it was finally past on to God's chosen people of Islam, the descendent of Abraham through Ishmael, past on to them by their great prophet Mohammed. What is this eternal message that is practiced by all three religious faiths? I will tell you. *"...You will be my people and I will be your God"* (Eze. 36: 28). This is the eternal message. By accepting God you accept his laws and you make a covenant with him, we will be his children and he will be our God (Father). The Moslem prays to God (Ala) five times each day and the opening statement before each prayer is "Come and pray to God who is God."

In the time of Moses as he wrote the book of Leviticus he states *"I am the Lord your God that brought you out of the land of Egypt and you shall be my people and I will be your God."*(Lev. 11:45) This statement in repeated in Lev. 22: 33 and Lev. 25:38 and in Num. 13:41. In the time of Jeremiah when Israel was being warned to repent and to forsake the Canaanite gods and return to the God of Abraham, God *said " But I commanded them to obey me, so that I would be their God and they would be my people"* (Jere. 7:23).

Today our society have advanced to the point that most civilized people do not worship any idol gods anymore but have elevated there consciousness to the understanding of a one, true, universal, all wise and all powerful monastic God, invisible, yet real. But the message of God remains the same, accept my laws and obey my words and make a covenant with me and you shall become my people and I will be your God. Think about it. How many people today sit down and truthfully make a private and personal covenant with God? Sit down now and pray to God, open your heart and make a covenant with God, a covenant of obedience to the law and to his will. Do this now and become one of his chosen people. The Eternal Message is "You will be my people and I will be your God."

Without fully knowing or seeing God we still have come to love him. I say now, without God in our life, we are but incomplete human beings. For his Spirit lives within us, and it gives us life and our Soul reflects his image and likeness.

Article Four
The Holy Scriptures

Brothers and Sisters, this book is the most talked about, the most studied, the most analyzed, and the most published book in the world. It is a book about God, the spiritual nature of man, and about angels. Also it is a book about Jesus, the Son of God, his passion, death, and resurrection, and God plan of Salvation. The Bible is a book that teaches high moral principles. It is held to be a Holy book reverence and respected by a billion people all over the world. Now can a billion people all be wrong or in error?

The Bible is a holy spiritual book that comes to us from God, and holds within it certain powers of transformation that brings about change. It builds character, makes ones thoughts and action noble and with honor. It teaches us to face up to our responsibilities, to be fair in our daily dealings and to be just in making our life decisions. Its laws and principles bring balance into our world of confusion and establish a world of order. It teaches us what is right and what is wrong, and it explains to us what is good, and what is evil.

World Without

I can't imagine living in a world without the Bible, for it has given us so much. Our world would become a world of chaos, full of evil. Without the Bible high moral teaches and standards of living we would live, in a world of hate, anger, murder, rape, stealing, adultery, a world of doom. You may say that I am wrong, and this could not really happen. Yet, we live in a world that does have the Bible and do we not witness such evil doings now.

The Bible say "Thou shall not kill (or murder), if we live in a world without this high moral teaching, then we would be allowed to murder and kill, without gilt, shame, or punishment, developing within us a nature of having no respect for life at all. The Bible teaches moral standards for family life including moral on sex. To live in a world without such guidelines would create a world such as Hitler tried to create with the results of millions of human being murdered and others killed. Any man can rape any woman without punishment, shame or guilt. The crime rate would increase because stealing would be allowed. This is something to think about.

Our whole Western society is founded upon God's Ten Commandments found in the Bible that helps our society maintain order and discipline. Our culture, traditions, and customs are derived from what God taught through the prophets found in the Bible. We all can learn much through the study of the Holy Scriptures.

The Goodness and Richness

"All scriptures are given by inspiration of God, and are profitable for doctrine, for reproof, for correction, for instruction in righteousness." II Timothy 3:16

The Holy Bible teaches many things such as history, other created beings, times and seasons, moral standards, stories of adventures, astronomy, physics, biology, philosophy, and much more. The Apostle Paul explains it correctly to Timothy in II Timothy 3:16

1. **Profitable:** The Holy Scriptures is profitable in learning correct teachings on faith in God, and daily life activities. We can profit in the spiritual life when we follow God's teaching. Storing up treasurers in heaven. It is profitable for obtaining knowledge and wisdom.

2. **Reproof:** The Holy Scriptures tells us what is right and what is wrong, and informs us or reproves us when we do something wrong. It makes us a shame when we do something we know is wrong.

3. **Correction:** The Holy Scriptures corrects us when we are in error. When we do something wrong and teaches us the correct way. It inspires us the correct things about God.

4. **Instruction:** The Holy Scriptures instructs us on salvation, righteous living, prayer, and the spiritual things about God. It gives us instruction on good healthy family living. Also there is proper instruction's on how to handle money so we don't have to live in debt, homeless, poor.

Other Benefits

1. **Hope:** The Holy Scriptures gives us hope for a better world, without pain and suffering, without death and sorrow. Now what is wrong with this?

2. **Diet:** The Holy Scriptures instructs us in proper diet that keeps us healthy and strong. Yet, so many Christian make the mistake in thinking that the dietary laws in the Old Testament are only for the Jews. Not so, it's a diet designed for and given to the whole human race.

3. **Love:** The Holy Scriptures teaches us the true meaning of "Love" how to love, and the results of true love. It instructs us on friendship and the blessing of having friends, the development of positive and meaningful relationships, and the blessing of children and the joy they bring.

4. **Wisdom:** The Holy Scriptures gives us knowledge and makes us wise on the spiritual things of our universe. It opens up our eyes to the truth of our existence, our spiritual nature, and our origin.

5. **Purpose:** The Holy Scriptures gives us a purpose in life and helps us understand what that purpose is. We are lost souls searching for a reason to life, and what it's all about, because we are without purpose and meaning.

6. **Eternal Message:** The Holy Scriptures tells of a war in heaven between good and evil, and how that war continues to this day here on earth. It tells us of the eternal message and that the Lord our God is the only true high God and we are his created beings.

Show Thyself Approved

"Study to shew thyself approved unto God, a workman that needeth not to be ashamed, rightly dividing the word of truth." II Timothy 2:15

I have designed a number of Bible study courses to help you and others in understanding God and what studying the Bible is all about. Learn all that can you learn from the Holy Scriptures.

Warnings for Biblical Scholars

Today we have two classes of Biblical scholars; the first is from the secular circle that teaches in colleges and universities, who are not really true, believers in Christ. They tent to be confused and have a misunderstanding of the interpretation of the Holy Scriptures. They also tent to pass on their misunderstanding and error to their students. This result graduates coming out of the university who teach error thanks to the influence of non-believing biblical scholars who were their teachers?

The second class of Biblical scholars is the seminary scholars who believe in the Bible, Christ, and in his teaching. I personally trust these scholars and would study under their guidance. These support and defend the Bible and the Christian faith.

Example: there are a group of Biblical scholars that are secular teachers that teach in university, who are voting on what Jesus real said in the Gospels. Can you believe this? Biblical scholars, 2000 yeas later voting on what Jesus truly said, I think this is laughable. Most scholars in the world don't agree with this small little group of confused scholars. These are the one's we need to become aware of that Jesus spoke of teaching beliefs, ideas, and errors, because they are doctrine of men "Be in vain they who worship me, teaching for doctrines the commandments of men." Matthew 15:9

Stay with the teaching of main stream Christianity, and stay away from strange doctrines "Be not carried about with divers and strange doctrines." Hebrew 13: 9 The New Testament is full of warnings about false prophets and teachers "But there were false prophets also among the people, even as there shall be false teachers among you, who privily shall bring in damnable heresies, even denying the Lord that bought them, and bring upon themselves swift destruction." II Peter 2:1

In Conclusion

Death is a sure thing, and no one can escape from it. It's a truth that no one can deny, it will happen. In our world we get old and the chances of suffering pain and discomfort is great. However, the Holy Scriptures testify to the resurrection of Jesus called the Christ, the holy one, the Messiah, the only one who ever conquered death. He lives to this day, and having faith in him, accepting him as your personal Savior; you are promised victory over the final death.

The teachings of the Holy Scriptures have timeless issues that have stood test of time, as they were recorded then, they stand true today. We may live in a technological world and our society has come a long way since Moses time, but human nature is the same, it has not change. We still suffer the pain that King David did, we still experience brother rivalry as Joseph did, make the same mistake that

Jacob did, experience adventures as Abraham did. We can relate to these stories we read in the Bible.

Article Five
Canonized Scriptures

It is the year 2006 and we are in the first decade of the seventh millenium since creation and two-millenium after the birth of our Lord and Saviour Jesus Bar Joseph, the Christ. Forty-six years ago our society enters into what was called the "Sexual" revolution, where life was care free and open. The young people in our world rebelled against the Vietnam War, against the established government, and against the authority of the Church. Because of this rebellion the tradition and teaching of the church was not past on to the next generation of young people. This led to a generation of non-believers, having no understanding, knowledge or faith in God.

We are facing the birth of the third generation of non-believers, and many of the first generation who took part of the sexual revolution is now professors teaching in our colleges and universities. Spreading atheism among our children who were born of parents that did not take part of the rebellion of the sixty's. We face an era where the Bible is attacked more than ever before by people who are trying to discredit the Bible and show others that there is no God.

Now, many of the old Gnostic writings (books) of the ancient world that were rejected by the early church fathers and were not part of the canonized collection of books that make up the Bible we use today are being republished. Their false theological teachings are now adding to the confusion that many Christians are being faces with in our world today. We need to hold fast to what we know to be true and reject those teachings we know to be false.

The Ecclesiastical Church

It was the early church fathers who formed the ecclesiastical church that gather together in a world council to review, discuss, and debate which books should be included in the canonized collection of books that will make up our Bible. This process did not take a week or two complete but centuries of research and debating. Bishop around the world was compiling lists of books they thought should be included in the canons.

In 367 AD St. Athanasius of Alexandria, Egypt wrote a letter to all the church under his protected authority along with a list of books he instructed should be accepted as authoritative canonized books. He was the first bishop to compile a list of books that make up the books of the New Testament that match our canonized New Testament 100 percent.

No scholar knows what guidelines the church fathers used in judging which book is inspired by God and which book are not. There are no written reports, notes, or letters we can use to find out. Scholars can only guess and offer opinions as to what guideline that the early church father used. I am no different than any other scholar, and can only offer my opinion. The following guideline I believed was used by the church fathers; however, I can be wrong.

1. I believe that the church father considered only those books written in the first century between 40 AD to 95 AD.

2. I believe that only those books written by the twelve apostles themselves who were eye witness, or by those companion of the apostles

3. Books that had the authors name written in the beginning of the opening paragraph that was the custom in the ancient world.

4. Books known through oral tradition to be written by apostles of Jesus.

5. Letters written by an author who declared that Jesus visited them in a vision, such as the Apostle Paul.

6. Books that conform to the theological teachings of Paul in his epistles and are not contradicting or present confusion.

Whatever guideline was used by the early church fathers to canonize the Bible it was done with many prayers, and held great responsibility in determining what books were inspired and which books were not. Among the three hundreds bishops, the Holy Spirit had to guide them into the set of right choices.

Jesus Christ founded the church and his message of salvation was cared throughout the world by his apostles. The church came first and the church received its authority from Peter. For Jesus gave Peter the Keys of the kingdom of heaven *"For you Peter are the rock in which I will build my church. I will give you the keys of the kingdom of heaven and what ever you bind on earth shall be bound in heaven. And what ever you allow on earth will be allowed in heaven."* (Matthew 16:19).

The First Order of Divinity

"The Holy Scriptures"

I John Paul, a Servant of Christ Jesus, by the grace of God, write this commentary on *the Holy Scriptures.* My blessings go with you. Peace from God our Father and from our Lord and Saviour Jesus of Nazareth called the Christ. The Holy Scriptures is the collection of sixty-six books, written under the inspiration of the Holy Spirit and is acknowledge by the Church as the true words of God. The writings of the Holy Scriptures are the mysterious workings of God and man. Through divine intervention the Creator has given us an inspirational book called the Bible.

Knowledge of the Holy Scriptures:

(1:1) Christ, divided the Old Testament.

Jesus Says "*That all things must be fulfilled which were written in the laws of Moses, and in the Prophets and in the Psalms, concerning me.*" Luke 24:44,45

Commentary: Jesus here points out the three divisions of the Old Testament, The Law, The Prophets, and the Psalms. And speaks of them as making up the Holy Scriptures, the Old Testament. By doing this he confirms the Old Testament as being the word of God. Since the foundation of the world was first created, God set in motion the Salvation of the world, which runs through the entire Old Testament writings.

The Law of Moses*:* That part of the Old Testament that was written by Moses, known as the Hebrew Torah commonly called the "PENTATEUCH" among Biblical Scholars of the Christian church, meaning five scrolls. The Law of Moses consists of the first five- (5) books of the Old

Testament (Genesis, Exodus, Leviticus, Numbers, and Deuteronomy). Elsewhere it is referred to as "The Law" (Matt. 7:12 and Luke 16:16), The Law of Moses (Acts 28:23) or just Moses (Luke 16:29,31). In the Gospel of Luke 24:44 is the only place in the Bible where specific reference to the division of the scripture is made also recognized by the Jewish people themselves.

The law of Moses written by Moses, but dictated by God, set down various ethical and moral laws which should still be obeyed and practice out of respect and love for God. Also are the Jewish sacrificial laws, which were done away by Christ when he died on the cross for the sins of the world. Jesus death was the ultimate sacrifice for the sins of the world. When Christ died, the curtain of the temple was torn from top to bottom in two, as if an angel of the Lord did it. This is the sign of the end of animal sacrifice.

The Prophets*:* The Jewish scholars today divide this section up into two categories, 1. The former prophets, and 2.The latter prophets. The former prophets contain the books of Joshua, Judges, I and II of Samuel, I and II Kings, and I and II Chronicles. The latter prophets are put into two categories the major and minor prophets. The Major Prophets contain the books of Isaiah, Jeremiah, Ezekial, and the twelve Minor Prophets are Hosea, Joel, Amos, Obadiah, Jonah, Micah, Nahum, Habakkuk, Zephaniah, Haggai, Zechariah, and Malachi that's listed in the Hebrew arrangement of the Old Testament.

In the Jewish Palestinian Bible the books of I and II Samuel and I and II Kings, and I and II Chronicles are counted each as one book each instead of six individual books like that of the Christian Bible. The books of the twelve Minor Prophets are also collected together as one book. There are 24 books that make up the Hebrew arrangement of the Old Testament in the Jewish Bible.

The Psalms*:* This section not only includes the book of psalms, but also other books which are not attributed to the writings of Moses or belong to the prophets. These books of the third section are commonly called *"Hagiographa"* or simply the writings. They are Ruth, Song of Solomon, Ecclesiastes, Lamentations, Proverbs, and Job,

Divine things and Spiritual knowledge

"The secrete things belong unto the Lord our God: but those things which are revealed belong unto us and to our children forever." Deuteronomy 29:29

"The secretes of the Lord is with them that show reverence to him, and he will show them the secretes of the promises." Psalms 25:14

Commentary: The Spirit of the Lord shall come upon you and will open your eyes as he did mine and you will receive understanding from your studies. To study the Holy Scriptures is to know God and to understand his mysteries. The study of "Theology" is the study of God, and it can be a long process. When you have a readiness of mind and an open and steady heart, then understanding will come to you.

This is why many people don't away agree upon a single point of doctrine, because both are not the same in having a readiness of mind. One may have understanding while the other can't understand because they are not ready to understand. In times like this patience must be stressed.

All things come in time, and the secret is to always continue your study, pray for guidance, and when the time is right, understanding will come.

(1:2) The apostles writings are part of the Holy Scriptures

"...Even as our beloved brother Paul also according to the wisdom given unto him hath written unto you; as also in all his epistles, speaking in them of these things; in which are some things hard to be understood, which they that are unlearned and unstable wrest, as they do also the other scriptures, unto their own destruction." II Peters 3:15, 16

Commentary: Peter here considers the apostle Paul and his writings as part of the scriptures, and doubtless he felt the same about the writings of the other apostles. Much of the beauty and depth of divine truth is lost to those who read only the New Testament. Jesus and his disciples preached, quoted, and taught the scriptures entirely from the Old Testament. Since they were the only sacred writings available. There is complete harmony between the Old and New Testament. They are a united, standing and falling together. The old is the foundation for the new. They are interwoven, heated, and welded in the fire of divine inspiration until they come to us as one divine inspired book.

The Old Testament and New Testament stand as two witnesses that remind us of the truth and reality of our world. Let no one confuse you, but test all things (teachings) and hold fast to those things you know and understand to be true.

"The sword of the spirit, which is the word of God."
Eph. 6:17

The Bible, the most talked about book, most analyzed book in history, yet it out sells all other books in the world. It is looked upon as a holy book of divine origin, and believed by billions around the world. The Bible holds within its pages the food that promotes and nourishes the spiritual life within us unto perfection.

How the Holy Scriptures were Written

(1:3) God holy words.

"All scriptures is given by inspiration of God and is profitable for doctrine, for reproof, for correction, for instruction in righteousness." II Timothy 3:16

Commentary: The key to understanding the scriptures lies in the proper translation of words which express God's correct thoughts on the sacred writings in general. Some scholars translate the first section of this verse to read as *"Every scripture inspired of God,"* or *"all inspired scripture"* or *"all scripture given by inspiration of God";* this is true for both, the Old and the New Testament. God did not give man the authority to differentiate what scriptures are of divine origin or made of man. The apostle Paul expands our thoughts on the scriptures as to the profitable rewards they contain and the four basic categories.

Doctrine: The word doctrine mean teaching. The Bible alone carries the knowledge in obtaining salvation. Only God, through grace, can offer man salvation. The Holy Scriptures explains our duty to our fellow man, and our duty to God. All of man's history and responsibility to God is recorded in the Scriptures.

It from the Holy Scriptures we develop theological theories, teachings, concepts, ideas, and dogma of the church. These theological developments inspired by God and they illuminate our soul with new knowledge and understanding.

Reproof: Translated from the Greek "Elegmos" which means censure. The Bible does both, it censures the sinner and provides a means of proving the scriptures to believers, and to weed out any perverted teachings.

Because it teaches us right from wrong, and shows us our ways of error and reproofs (corrects) us in the things that we done wrong.

Correction: The Bible will show us the right path which leads to God, and the wrong things we do which prevents our efforts to reach God. We, by the power of free choice, may choose the path we so wish to follow. By pointing out our wrong doings, it also offers correction and to make things right. Allowing us to improve ourselves by giving up those bad habits and sinful acts we loved and enjoyed. By accepting and practicing what the Bible teaches, it will manifest its transforming powers, and bring about a transformation in our lives, and initiate us into the holy family of God.

Instruction: The Holy Scriptures gives us discipline. It trains us, just as if we were children being taught the basic responsibilities of adulthood. So we learn from the scriptures the special instruction in living a healthy and proper Christian life.

Many people get the wrong idea about the teachings and instruction the Bible gives us. They are not given to please God, but for our salvation. They are given so we can improve our health, find inner peace and harmony. They are given for our benefit. They have been given to us so we may learn about our Creator and about the universe he created. To learn about nature and the great love that is poured out for us.

Many of the so-called reborn Christian go overboard on their Christian life to the point where they place upon themselves so many demanding restrictions that it turns off many other people who wish to become Christian. Religion like anything else in life must maintain a balance. Some people take religion too far and are given the nickname "Holy Rollers," I call them fanatics. They take always the love and fun of worshiping God. Each Church (Catholic or Protestant) that places upon its member more demands and discipline than the Bible calls for or that God requires of you, is in error, and makes it hard for its members to practice the faith.

Note: Beware, do not let yourself be brainwashed by your priest, minister, or ecclesiastical and fundamental teachers to the point that you are unable to think for yourself with an open mind. Do not allow yourself to become a blind follower. Do not allow anyone to take away your freedom to study with an open mind, your right for free thinking, and your right to question, challenge, to do research, and to confirm what you accept to be true.

Another problem with fundamental Christian is that, those things that they don't fully understand, they label as being Satanic, without proper investigation or explanation. I truly feel sorry for those people and pray that none of my students will ever fall into this type of religion, for they will restricted your ability to search out the truth and fine enlightenment.

Be careful how you study, interpret, and draw conclusion on the teachings of Christ, and the fundamental principles of Salvation.

(1:4) God inspired holy men.

"For the prophecy came not in old time by the will of man; but holy men of God spake as they were moved by the Holy Spirit." II Peter 1:21

Commentary: Special men who were chosen by God to reveal his divine message and teachings, were moved by the Holy Spirit, by a method known as "Empathy." This is a method by which both the chosen person and the Holy Spirit become one in thoughts and in feelings. At this point the prophet or apostle of the Lord becomes elevated in thought and spirit and is given a profound sense of understanding.

This is a method I believe that God used upon His prophets and the apostles. Being in a state of harmony and enlighten understand wrote down the things God inspired them through their own personally and style using their own vocabulary. Thus making the thought behind the word as being inspired of God and not the word, itself, because today translated can use many different kinds of words to express God's thoughts.

The Holy Spirit came upon these prophets and the two became as one, one emotion and feeling, one in thought, one in purpose, ideal, goal, and plan, one in action. A special unity, relationship existed between the Creator (God) and His creature (Man). This was not a form of control, but one of mutual love, respect, and understanding.

God's Purpose and Reason

(1:5) The Holy Scriptures profitable.

"And that from a child thou has known the Holy Scriptures, which are able to make thee wise unto salvation through faith which is in Christ Jesus" II Timothy 3:15-17

Commentary: Through the study of the Holy Scriptures we can learn all about Salvation, our origin, Satan and his evil angels, and about Jesus Christ, plus much, much more. The Holy Scripture gives us knowledge of the mystery of God, the deep secrete things of God. The Holy Scriptures is very profitable, for it changes lives, it brings joy and hope into people lives. It help's make our world a better place to live.

(1:6) Jesus in the Scriptures.

"Search the scriptures; for in them ye think ye have eternal life: and they are they, which testify of me." St. John 5:39

"And beginning at Moses and all the prophets, he expounded unto them in all the scriptures the things concerning himself." St. Luke 24:27

Commentary: Jesus was telling the people of his day that though they were searching the scriptures diligently (Daily) in quest of eternal life, they had misunderstood the prophecies they had read about the Messiah. They did not recognize the Creator Son, Jesus Christ, who was even then standing among them.

The Jewish people of Jesus time believed that knowledge of the law would itself assure them eternal life. Rabbi Hillel stated in the first century BCE, "One who has acquired unto himself words of Torah, has acquired for itself the life of the world to come" (Mishnah Aboth 2.7 Soncinoed) Talmud. If the Jews, in the time of Christ would search the Scriptures with eyes of faith, those scriptures that were written of the Messiah, they would have recognized Jesus as the Messiah as he stood among them.

However, we must realize that the Jews in Jesus time was a nation of salves under the controlling rule of the Romans, and was given a life of hardship, high taxes, and lost of self identities. This type of life has gone on for decades, and its no wonder why the Jewish people looked for a powerful King Messiah that would over throw the Romans empire and save them. Many times we see in the scriptures what we desire most and lose sight of what Scriptures really is teaching.

How to study the Scriptures

(1:7) A Biblical way of studying the Holy Scriptures.

"These were more noble than those in Thessalonica, in that they received the word with all readiness of mind, and searched the scriptures daily, whether those things were so." Acts 17:11

Commentary: The people of Berea were nobler than other Christian churches because they searched the scriptures daily to test the new teachings of Paul. To see if what he was telling them was true and of divine origin. The people of Berea used their intelligence when they studied the scriptures. With eyes of faith found the inspired words, which told of the Messiah. Once they review all the facts and evidence, they eagerly accepted the truth Paul was teaching, thereby proving their sincerity.

They studied the Holy Scriptures with readiness (open) of mind and learn the truth. They search the scriptures and found salvation through Jesus Christ. I think there faith enable them to become theological advance more than the other Churches. They could not be carried by the winds of confusion, but rooted them selves in the words of God.

(1:8) Spiritual guidance for understanding

"But God hath revealed them unto us by his spirit: for the spirit searcheth all things, yea, the deep things of God, for what man knoweth the things of a man, save the spirit of man which is in him? Even so the things of God knoweth no man, but the spirit of God." I Corinthians 2:10,11

Commentary: God has prepared a plan where we can continue receiving God's revelation of truth through his Holy Scriptures. The understanding of spiritual knowledge, the spiritual things of God, is given to and understood by those people who truly love God, and is spiritually open to the Holy Spirit. Those people who are in spiritual union with God, appreciate the Love God has poured out for them. Those who are good Christians accept whatever provision God has made for them and are happy to search the divine truth in all things, and are busy storing their real treasure in heaven.

It is through the working of the Holy Spirit, the third person of the Godhead, that guide us, by influencing us and moves us to study and understanding the Holy Scriptures. This is why good Bible studied pray before each study or reading of the Holy Scriptures for guidance and understanding.

"But the comforter, which is the Holy Spirit, whom the Father will send in my name, he shall teach you all things, and bring all things to your remembrance, whatsoever I have said unto you." Apostle John 14:26

Because he is a member of the Godhead, the Holy Spirit knows all things. It is the work of the Holy Spirit to bring the spiritual things of God to our understanding, then later to our remembrance and guide us into various mysteries. With the help of the Holy Spirit we are better able to investigate the truth with an honest open heart.

"Howbeit when he, the Spirit of Truth, is come, he will guide you into all truth: for he shall not speak of himself; but whatsoever he shall hear, that shall be speak: and he will show you things to come. He shall glorify me: for he shall receive of mine, and shall show it unto you." John 16:14

(1:9) Chosen Teachers.

"Go ye therefor, and teach all nations, Baptize them in the name of the Father, and of the Son, and of the Holy Spirit; Teaching them to observe all things whatsoever I have commanded you: and lo, I am with you always even unto the end of the world." Matt. 28:19, 20

Commentary: Once we have fully learned the Scriptures we slowly begin to understand God's plan for man's salvation. It is our Christian duty to go out and make disciples of all nations. We do this by living the example of Christian life. We don't go out and force God's teaching upon anyone. Just live the Christian life and your example of joy and happiness will interest non-believers, and they will then approach you and ask, that's when you share the good news of the Gospels.

The proper way of studying the Holy Scriptures is through the guidance of your Church, or by an educated scholar or teacher. It has been my belief that no one person should study the Holy Scriptures by them selves. Read it by your self yes, but not study it and interpret it by your self. It's too easy for Satan to interject error into your mind. Everyone needs a teacher and study partner. Some people will say that I can study by myself with the help of the Holy Spirit. It is by this method why we have so many different branches (Churches) of Christianity. But remember what Jesus said. *"Where two or more are gathered in my name, there shall I be."* (Mathew 18:20). It is too easy to come across error, for a hundred people that study by themselves will come up with a hundred different teachings. This is not the working of the Holy Spirit.

Example: In the early church a council of bishops from around the world is called to discuss doctrine of the church, each bishop has two biblical scholar to advise him, one an expert in Greek and one an expert in Hebrew. When 316 bishops write the "Nicene Creed" and agree upon it, that is the working of the Holy Spirit. This is how we preserve the truth, the teachings of the apostles and our Christian heritage. The Protestant Churches all follow the same system of preserving the teachings of God. When you do a religious survey of all the various Christian Churches, you will find very little deference between them, and the small deference you do find has nothing to do with salvation. So I advise you. Make Jesus your center of focus when studying the Bible, so that you may obtain salvation.

Once you find a Biblical teacher (scholar) that you are comfortable with, then learn, study, and find true joy in it. As you step out in faith and accept the teaching of God, you will embrace it with your entire mind and heart, and people will know you who you are when you practice the faith. Remember, know and understanding the Holy Scriptures is not enough. You must practice what you are taught. You must practice what you tell others. You must live the example of a joyous Christian Life.

When you accept Jesus Christ as your Saviour, you will want to follow in his footsteps, follow and practice his teachings; you will find great joy in living the Christian life the way Christ taught it.

Jesus Christ, through his Gospels, commissions every Christian to go forth and share the good news, and the teachings of the Holy Scriptures. However, we are warned against false teachings and teachers who teach them. God has given us a standard by which we my Judge the teaching of every man.

"To the law and to the testimony: if they speak not according to this word, it is because there is no light in them." Isaiah 8:20

The Holy Spirit's guidance

(1:10) Receiving the Holy Spirit guidance.

"And I say unto you, ask, and it shall be given you; seek, and ye shall find; knock, and the door shall be opened unto you." Luke 11:9

Commentary: All we have to do is ask, and our heavenly Father will send the Holy Spirit to us. For what father will bring harm to his son and daughter when they come and asks for help?

"If ye then, being evil, know how to give good gifts unto your children: how much more shall your heavenly Father give the Holy Spirit to them that ask him? Luke 11:13

(1:11) Bible students are called.

"For as many as are led by the spirit of God, they are the Sons of god." Romans 8:14

Commentary: Are you willing to allow yourself to be guided by the Holy Spirit? At various times in your life you will experience a real battle or conflict within your self. It is the classic conflict between good and evil. Here you will experience what every child of God knows to be true "The battle within" the struggle of your stubborn will and a rebellious heart against God's divine wisdom and loving nature. These are the things we need to overcome, by using the power within all of us. The guidance of the Holy Spirit is not just a momentary impulse, but a steady flow of blessings and graces, spiritual influences, protection, healing, strength and of inspirational thoughts.

It is very important to understand that the guidance of the Holy Spirit is not to be taken in a way that will imply that we are being forced against our free will. We still have the power of free choice. The transforming power of the Holy Spirit will come only when you open your heart. The Holy Spirit will dwell only in the hearts of those who accept him in faith. Your faith is the proof that you are a loving and willing disciple of truth, an obedient child of God, accepting the Lords will, and also accepting the spiritual influence and guidance of the Holy Spirit.

Reference: *"And we are his witness of these things; and so is also the Holy Spirit, whom God hath given to them that obey him."* Acts 5:32

Commentary: God's only requirement for receiving the Holy Spirit is obedience to the Holy Spirit influence. The obedience of a creature to the will of his Creator is the religious foundation of all faith. We enter into a special relationship with God, a unity, only when we ourselves become obedient to his will. The Angels of God also obey his will.

Reference: *"Bless the Lord, ye his angels, that excel in strength, that do his commandments, heartening unto the voice of his word."* Psalms 103:20

The Angels of the Lord obey and follow God out of love and not from fear or legal formality. When a father asks his child to do a special job, the obedient and loving child does it, out of respect, love, and faith. So when the Holy Spirit influences us to obey God's will, we do it out of love, respect, and faith. Men are also instructed to obey God like the angles.

"Let us hear the conclusion of the whole matter: Fear God, and keep his commandments: for this is the whole duty of man." Ecclesiastes 12:13

Commentary: Out of fear comes respect which in time turns into understanding and then finally it becomes love. By the commandments we come to known sin, and as a reborn Christian, through baptism we become a new person in Christ and we forsake our sins.

"If ye love me, keep my commandments." John 14:15

Commentary: When Jesus died for us on the cross, he did not do away with the law, but gave us a clear understanding of the law. What Jesus did away was the understanding that salvation (become right with God) can be obtained by obeying the law. Now its faith in Jesus Christ, for his blood paid the ultimate price for the salvation of the soul.

"If any man will do his will, he shall know of the doctrine, whether it be of God, or whether I speak of myself." John 7:17

"I understand more than the ancients, because I keep thy precepts." Ps. 119:100

Commentary: We keep the laws of God, not to obtain salvation, but because we love God and in our effort to understand God's law, we find sweetness and joy in being obedient, for salvation comes only through faith in our Lord Jesus, called the Christ.

Decree of the Church

1. In his encyclical letter *"Providintissimus Deus,"* Pope Leo XIII set up guidelines in studying, researching and interpreting the Holy Scriptures. Nov. 18, 1893

2. Pope Benedict XV writes in his encyclical letter *"Spiritus Paraclitus"* Sept. 15, 1920 "All the children of the Church, especially the priesthood, should respect and reverence the Holy Scriptures, and to humbly read it and meditate upon the sacred books constantly."

3. "We must use every endeavor that the "Word of God" may dwell in us abundantly." St. John Chrysostom in his book on the priesthood.

The Second Order of Divinity

"Sound Doctrine"

I John Paul, a Servant of Christ Jesus, by the grace of God, do write this commentary on *Sound Doctrine.* My blessings go with you. Peace from God our Father and from our Lord and Saviour Jesus of Nazareth called the Christ. The Holy Bible is your textbook of spiritual knowledge about righteous living. It is sound doctrine, which light the path to salvation and spiritual revelation. So the value of Bible studies cannot be over estimated. Knowledge of its teachings, history, and principles is an essential preparation to everyone who has received the calling to become a disciple (followers) of Christ, a priest of the priesthood and ministers and teachers, or a Biblical Scholar of God's holy words. As children of God and followers of Jesus Christ we are to read and study the Holy Scriptures daily, and I would add to this the "Nine Orders of Divinity," and other future volumes I may write.

Instruction from Paul

Searching out the truth and laying down a strong foundation for your spiritual growth. You can not allow yourself to be moved, when another wind (teaching) blows by, spreading the doctrine of men. St. Paul writes in his second letter to timothy.

"Study to show thyself approved unto God, a workman that needeth not to be ashamed, rightly diving the word of truth." II Timothy 2:15

One of our duties as Christians is to share the salvation of our Lord to everyone who come to us and ask us for spiritual help. St. Paul reminds us that only earnest and diligent students can rightly represent the Lord in this work.

Besides teaching and sharing the salvation of the Lord, we must live the example of our teaching. We must show ourselves as true Christians. Sound Doctrine means that the truth of the Bible must be properly interpreted so no part of the Holy Scriptures will be set in opposition to the general teachings of the Holy Bible as a whole.

The knowledge of the Holy Scriptures as taught by the Early Church is certainly one of the most necessary points of the Christian faith. Because the Holy Scriptures is the foundation of our faith, and the early Christian Church is entrusted as the guardian and protector of that faith. By which we can come to know God through the guidance of the Holy Spirit into the true interpretation of the Holy Scriptures.

The Sacred Scriptures

(2:1) The Holy Scriptures Teaches.

> *"For whatsoever things were written aforetime were written for our learning, that we through patience and comfort of the Scriptures might have hope."* Romans 15:4

Commentary: The Scriptures are given for our learning, for our instruction. St. Paul knew that his letters were being collected and compiled by some of the churches, even in his day. Yet, he looked upon the Old Testament as a collection of writings, compiled for moral instruction and guidance, and would continue to hold its place among the many other sacred books and writings of the world.

The sacred Scriptures inspires us, comforts us, and gives us hope in being a part of the Kingdom of Heaven. It gives us hope so we may endure the suffering for God and our fellow man. The early Christians displayed great endurance, they showed the world and set us an example of how to accept the hardship of life, and the comfort that the Holy Scriptures provides for us in time of suffering. This confirms and strengthens us, and gives us hope, thereby showing us that we have stood the test.

(2:2) God's Divine plan.

"That the man of God may be perfect, thoroughly furnished unto all good works." II Timothy 3:17

Commentary: Only those open minded Christians can exercise their freedom of choice, and sincerely allow the Holy Spirit to work in them through the sacred Scriptures you can rightly be called the sons of God. Through daily study of the Holy Scriptures a transformation will take place and the students of God will become spiritually perfect, complete, thoroughly furnished. A teaching of God for all Christians to expire to and become completely fitted and equipped with the words of truth. To be blessed with the knowledge of God, is the highest honor man was ever given. To be entrusted with the knowledge of the Bible and communicate its treasures to the entire world.

(2:3) The Character of God.

"He is the rock, his work is perfect: for all his ways are judgement: A God of truth and without iniquity, just and right is he." Deuteronomy 32:4

Commentary: We can learn much by reviewing the meaning of certain words in the above verse. The character of God holds many elements; such are these that follow.

Rock: God is the only true rock, a solid foundation that is unchanging in nature. A foundation that will endures forever.

Perfect: He himself is perfect, never leaving any of his work unfinished or imperfect. He will carry out the salvation of man to its perfected end. God is perfect in all ways and when we imitate Him we our selves slowly unfold unto spiritual perfection, and come to know him intimately.

Truth: Being a Creator, his works, actions, and words stand as universal truth, He is God. He never goes back on his word, and his truth is sure.

Iniquity*:* A Creator without iniquity (sin) for it is impossible for the nature of God to be evil, to be wrong, or to be unjust. This is very hard for some people to understand this. He is Himself his own standard of action. He set us an example for all his people on how to live in harmony with his own divine attributes.

(2:4) God's words.

"Sanctify them through thy truth; thy words is truth.
St. John 17:17

Commentary: The word sanctify means "To make holy," "To consecrate," "To treat holy" and to "Set Aside," as holy. The Disciples of Christ are to be consecrated or made holy unto all good works before they go forth as teachers. Holiness is one of God's attributes.

Pastors, ministers, deacon, and Bible teachers are ordained and made holy, being set aside to do God's holy work. The reason is to make sure that the chosen person of God had truly received God calling to his ministry, and is properly trained and educated in God word. This is done to ensure that the shepherd is ready to watch over God's sheep. For it's a deep important responsibility to watch over God's people.

Bible Reference*: "Because it is written, be ye holy; for I am holy."* I Peters 1:16

Hence to be made holy is to become like God through the process of Sanctification. This is the foundation of Christian faith, that salvation is designed to elevate men to becoming a divine reflection of God's goodness, truth, and love.

Bible Reference*: "Whereby are given unto us exceeding great and precious promises: that by these ye might be partakers of the divine nature, having escaped the corruption that is in the world through lust."* II Peters 1:4

Partaking of God's divine nature. God's words are declared to be truth, the sacred Scriptures reveal to us the true character of God's words for we become new creatures by making the truth of God's words a part of our life.

We as human do have the ability to become one with God on a physical level that allows us to become partaker of God's divine nature. From a spiritual level, we can partake of God's divine nature through faith in Christ Jesus, become part of our spiritual nature, recorded upon the memory of our soul.

(2:5) God's words are magnified

"I will worship toward thy holy temple, and praise thy name for thy loving-kindness and for thy truth: for thou hast magnified thy word above all thy name." Psalms 138:2

Commentary: The name of God is the most Holiness of all names. The Old Jewish priests, prophets, and rabbis would not even say his name for it was looked upon as being very holy. The scribe themselves left the name of God out of the Scriptures and put "God" or "Lord" in its place because it was so Holy of a name. Here God's words are magnified above his own name because they are filled with power of truth. In ancient times, a man's name stood for his character. It was the same with God. When God placed his word above his name, his character becomes the foundation of his word.

His word has power because as God spoke the word, and created the earth and all things within, above, and below the earth. Through the working of the Holy Spirit, God words are then magnified (made clear) for our understanding.

Reference: "For when God made promise to Abraham, because he could swear by no greater, he swear by himself." Hebrew 6:13

(2:6) God's word stand forever.

"The grass withereth, the flower fadeth: But the word of God shall stand forever." Isaiah 40:18

Commentary: Man is a creature, created by God and is not immortal. Both the elements of man and of the grass (Vegetation) possess the same spiritual energy, which gives them both life. Both hold the same elements of the earth, and is able to sustain the physical means of the human body.

Both man and the animals along with all vegetation will die and pass away, but the word of God shall stand and live forever. The Bible reveals the will of God. It contains the written words, which carry His thoughts. These words become our spiritual food. Always remember that truth never changes, it stands today as it did yesterday and it shall stand forever.

"Jesus Christ the same yesterday, and today, and for ever."
Hebrew13:8

Any Christian who comes to him for the cleansing and sustaining of their inner spirit will never hunger.

"And Jesus said unto them, I am the bread of life; he that cometh to me shall never hunger; and he that believeth on me shall never thirst." St. John 6:35 nor will they thirst.

(2:7) God chosen us for Salvation.

"God hath from the beginning chosen you to salvation through sanctification of the spirit and belief of the truth." II Thessalonians 2:13

Commentary: Salvation is through faith in Jesus Christ, given to all as a free gift from God. It matters very much what we believe in and why God himself has chosen you unto salvation. Only by your sanctification through the works of the Holy Spirit, can you come to understand the spiritual things of God, and only then can you experience a spiritual change in your life. To be sincere is not enough. We must understand and know the truth. For only by the truth can we know the correct way, which leads to salvation. So sound doctrine does effect our lives. It can lead us to life or through incorrect doctrine it can lead us to death. No one would think to say that it is not important which road I travel on, so long as I think I am on the right road. To be Sincere is only a virtue, but it is not a proper test for sound doctrine.

It is God's will that we shall know the truth and such provision has been made, whereby we may know the truth. Follow the example of the church of Berea, who studied and check those things that others where teaching against what the Bible teaches. If both, the teaching of the Bible and the teaching of others (friends, pastor, elders, or another bible teacher) are in agreement with the same principle then you will know that the other person is teaching the truth, and is acceptable as doctrine.

(2:8) Joshua worships the true high God.

"Now therefore fear the Lord, and serve him in sincerity and in truth: and put away the gods which your fathers served on the other side of the flood, and in Egypt; and serve ye the Lord." Joshua 24:14

Commentary: Joshua was very particular whom his family or the nation of Israel should worship and serve. At the time, Joshua knew that even now idolatry was being secretly practiced by some of the Israelites. So he states in verse 15 that he and his family will worship and serve the Lord. There is only one true God and Him only shall we serve. The influence of all idolatrous worship is degrading.

"But I say, that the things which the Gentiles sacrifice, they sacrifice to devils, and not to God: and I would not that ye should have fellowship with devils." I Corinthians 10:20

Bible Reference: "Little children, keep yourselves from idols." I John 5:21

(2:9) Hold fast to sound doctrine.

"But speak thou the things which become sound doctrine. Titus 2:1

Commentary: In this chapter St. Paul tells of the three task confronting Titus. 1. He is to organize the Cretan Church (Verse 1:5); 2. To refute the vain talkers and deceivers (see verse 10) who were teaching unsound doctrine and degrading the moral tone of the Early Christian Church; and 3. To spread and communicate clearly and accurately the truth of the Gospel. Only those that are skilled and trained in the Holy Scriptures should teach the Gospel of Jesus Christ.

Men such as Apostles of Christ, Ordained priests and Ministers, Biblical Scholars and teachers, Rabbi, and Elders of the Church. Only these men have the authority from God and Church to speak on Sound Doctrine. Because of the importance in the salvation of the human soul, people and students should seek out a trained and educated person (man or woman) in the knowledge of the Bible, and teaching of the Holy Scriptures.

Only by allowing educated, trained and holy men to teach on Sound Doctrine can we safeguard the truth without error creeping in. Most lay people of the Church or the general public doesn't have college education or any Biblical training in Greek, Hebrew, Theology, Patrology, or general and in-depth Biblical education and training. It is too easy for people to start teaching their own opinions and ideas that are in error.

(2:10) Warnings against False Doctrine.

"That we henceforth be no more children, tossed to and fro, and carried about with every wind of doctrine, by the sleight of men, and cunning craftiness, whereby they lie in wait to deceive." Ephesians 4:14

Commentary: We are to become like little children in humility and truthfulness; but not to act on impulse and immaturity in learning new doctrine. We have to test each new teaching and allow all new teachings to face any opposition, and observe to see if it will stand the test or will it fall. We need to study its origin, if any. The object of God's blessing is as an infant in the light of new truth; we might grow up into spiritual adulthood. The Scriptures state that we should not be tossed to and fro. Christian who lacks the steadiness and is not rooted in the Holy Scriptures become weak believers; only patience, endurance, and stability are the true mark of a good and strong Christian.

Those people who are unhappy with what they have, will easily be influence to change and run with what ever comes along on impulse, things that interest them, or people that make great promises following new ideals and philosophy. So many people accept unproven ideas and theories as sound doctrine. These are the people who stand on feeble ground and have not rooted themselves in God's truth. Biblical, Theological, and philosophical teaching and speculations that go beyond legitimate limits makes for instability of belief and truth.

St. Paul warns us of the indecision, uncertainty and the vagueness that accompanies so much of our modern day theology. With the advent of Science, the church now needs to defend itself against the attaches by non-believers from the scientific community.

Bible Reference: "Be not carried about with divers and strange doctrines..." Hebrew 13:9

Commentary: Some Christians are easily influenced by any new or strange teaching, they lack the spiritual discrimination, they find it hard to differentiate between good and evil. What is false and what is truth. These people need to associate themselves with educated and well-trained true Christian of the mainstream churches, and learn from them.

(2:11) Rewards for teaching false doctrine.

"Who concerning the truth have erred, saying that the resurrection is past already; and overthrow the faith of some." II Timothy 2:18

Commentary: Paul writes to Timothy reminding him of the resurrection and how some teachers of the Christian faith denied the literal resurrection of the body (I Cor. 15:12-19). These men did not rightly divide the word of truth (verse 15). Because of this many teachers are teaching false doctrine. Also many Christian are content to accept the teaching of Church leaders and Biblical students, instead of diligently studying the Holy Scripture them selves. Because of the lack of study, whenever error comes in, they are lost to distinguish between it and the truth.

(2:12) Results from false teachings.

"But in vain they do worship me teaching for doctrines the commandments of men." Matthew 15:9

Commentary: Many false minister or misguided spiritual leaders and teachers will mislead many people, because they themselves are misguided. Other teachers out of vain or egotistical pride will teach their own doctrine (the teachings of men), and many people will become believers, faithfully following the commandments of men, but never obtaining the salvation of the Lord.

(2:13) False doctrine of the last days.

"Now the spirit speaketh expressly that in the latter times some shall depart from the faith, giving heed to seducing spirits, and doctrine of devils." I. Timothy 4:1

Commentary: In the latter days the devil will send out his seducing spirits to trick all or as many of God's faithful he can.

Spirit:: The Holy Spirit is speaking through St. Paul himself.

Depart:: From the Greek word *"Aphisteme,"* meaning, "To remove oneself from," "To Apostatize." St. Paul foretold of the apostasy of the Christian Church and how many will depart from the true teaching.

"Take heed therefor unto yourselves, and to all the flock, over the which the Holy Spirit hath made you overseers, to feed the Church of God, which he hath purchased with his own blood. For I know this, that after my departing shall grievous wolves enter in among you, not sparing the flock. Also of your own selves shall men arise, speaking perverse things, to draw away disciples after them." Act 20:28-30

Seducing: literally means "Wandering," hence misleading and deceptive. Many Christians will mix error with truth and mislead others from the Church.

Spirits: Seducing spirits influencing men.

"Beloved, believe not every spirit. But try the spirits whether they are of God: because many false prophets are gone out into the world." I John 4:1

Devils: From the Greek *"Daimonia"* meaning *"Demons."*

"But I say that the things, which the Gentiles sacrifice, they sacrifice to devils, and not to God: and I would not that ye should have fellowship with devils." I Cor. 10:20

These demons move men to believe their false doctrine than go out and become teachers of deception.

"Then entered Satan into Judas surnamed Iscariot, being of the number of the twelve." St. Luke 22:3

Satan works to control the minds of men, so it is very important to intellectually grasp the truth. Modern philosophies of occults, some metaphysics but not all, mystics, spiritualism, channeling, and out of body experience, are all examples of doctrine of devils. Pagan worship of animal and female gods, witchcraft (today nature worshippers), and demon deity worship, are real and are practiced today, more than ever.

Many of these old practices are being revived and practiced by modern day misguided, delusion people. Its seductive influence will eventually sweep the world Christian and non-Christian alike. When the time is right Satan will make his last great delusion in hopes of overthrowing the government of God.

Bible Reference: "But there were false prophets also among the people, even as there shall be false teachings among you, who privily shall bring in dammed heresies, even denying the Lord that brought them, and bring upon themselves swift destruction." II Peter 2:1

Commentary: Peter distinguishes between a prophet who claims to deliver God's message, and a teacher (Scholar) who interprets the message. He warns of the false teachers who has and more important who will arise, even among the true believers. St. Peter was told, as a Disciples of Christ to beware of false prophets.

(2:14) Guard ourselves against false teachers.

"Beware of false prophets, which come to you in sheep's clothing, but inwardly they are ravening wolves." Matthew 7:15

Commentary: There had been many false prophets in the Old Testament times, as in the time of the apostles and early church fathers. Even in our day, we have false people teaching you their own doctrine of men. Before the Second Coming of Christ there will be great false prophets working wondrous miracles.

Bible Reference: "Then the Lord said unto me, the prophets prophesy lies in my name: I sent them not neither have I commanded them, neither spake unto them: they prophesy unto you false vision and divination, and a thing of nought, and the deceit of their heart." Jeremiah 14:14

Peter gives an example of such false prophets and how people were moved to follow them.

"Which have forsaken the right way, and are gone astray, following the way of Balaam the son of Bosor, who loved the wages of unrighteousness." II Peter 2:15

Peter use of strong words like "heresies" is justified when he describes the things these teachers taught: 1. Denial of the Lord (verse 1) 2. Disregarding moral and sexual laws, and set standards (verses 10 and 18); and 3. Turning away from the Holy Commandments (verse 21).

(2:15) Men turn their ears to.

"For the time will come when they will not endure sound doctrine: But after their own lust shall they heap to themselves yeachers, having itching ears… and they shall turn away their ears from the truth, and shall all turned unto fables." II Timothy 4:3,4

Commentary: There is much to know in this verse. Let us review the key words and define their meaning, so we may get a clearer understanding.

Time will come*:* The apostle Paul undoubtedly knew of the time when the great falling away of the church would come (the apostasy), and would continue its false teaching until the Second Advent of Christ (read St. Matthew 24:23-27; Acts 20:28-31; Thessalonians 2:1-12; I Timothy 4:1-3 and II Timothy 3:1-5).

Endure*:* To listen willingly to false and unsound doctrines. We Christians receive strength and energy only when we hold within us the truth of the Lord. False interpretation of the Scriptures will bring about quarrels, strife, evil practices, and envy (I Timothy 6:3-6).

Itching ears*:* These are the people who do not endure sound doctrine, but follow after their own lust. People whose ears itch to hear false interpretation to justify their lust, sinful habits, and personal points of interest. Practicing the doctrine of men and not the true teachings of the Lord through curiosity and self desire they accept those scriptures which seem to approve their actions, but neglect the strong demands of sound doctrine, which cuts deep into our soul. They will only open their mind and ears to the teaching that will not disturb the daily routine of their perverted lives.

Truth: Many people will not endure sound doctrine, through the divine power of free choice they will choose their own destiny. It is not God's character to force anyone to accept his way. However, we as Christian willfully accept the Bible as our authoritative source for standards in religious teachings and moral conduct. Sound doctrine shows us the truth, exposes to us our error and sinful condition. It reveals correct ways of living. Truth reveals the nature of God's plan of salvation and brings inner peace and harmony. Unfaithful Christian will prepare and compile their own doctrinal theories in accordance with their desires (I Timothy 1:4).

Warning: Whenever Biblical text is used apart from their true original meaning, these types of teaching may prove to be unsafe for spiritual guidance.

The test of true and false doctrine

(2:16) Guideline for the truthfulness of any doctrine.

"Prove all things; hold fast that which is good." I Thessalonians 5:21

Commentary: We should be careful, and properly divide the false from the truth, specifically the manifestation of the spirit (see verse 19 and 20). God has provided us a definite method of testing new prophets and teachers. 1. A true prophets and teacher will confess Christ as the Saviour and Lord, and live it in his life and in his words (I John 4:1-3). 2. He will acknowledge the divinity of Christ (I John 2:22,23). 3. His teaching must be in harmony with that of the Holy Scriptures (Acts 17:11 and Galatians 1:8&9). 4. The end result of his teachings must show the fruitful harvest of all good things (St. Matthew 7:18-20). 5. He must profess the bodily resurrection of Christ (Matt. 28: 1-7, Mark 16: 1-6, and Luke 24: 39).

It is not enough to only test all spiritual gifts and believe in them. It is not enough to know what is false and what is true or what is evil and what is good. Once you have found the truth and good, and have established the strong foundation of your belief, you must hold on to it, retain it, in spite of all temptation to never let it go.

(2:17) Sound doctrine brings about inner change.

"Holding fast the faithful word as he hath been taught, that he may be able by sound doctrine both to exhort and to convince the gainsayers." Titus 1:9

Commentary: In any Christian religion, the highest calling is to the ministry of Christ. Our Lord Jesus Christ has instructed us to go forth and preach his Gospel. *"Go ye therefor and teach all nation"* St. Matthew 28:19 Every member of a Church or Parish is a minister for Christ, share his plan of salvation. But to become an ordained minister of God, this calling demands a compassionate heart of the highest order. Before his or her ordination, the minister must manifest the following ability.

1. The understanding of the teachings of the Holy Scriptures, of Sacred Tradition, and have studies the

writings of the Early Church Fathers and the Doctors of the Church.

2. The minister needs have the ability to communicate God's message to our fellow man. An understanding and compassionate heart.

3. Each minister does God's ministry according to the gifts given to him by God. He must devote himself to the daily prayer and to the study of the Holy Scriptures.

The ministry of the Lord will have more demands upon himself than any other profession. The need for continuing education never ends. Our ministry is more than a profession; it is a divine calling.

Note: The meaning of the word gainsayers in this verse "Those people who speak against," another definition is "The contradicter."

Our Personal Attitude toward Truth

(2:18) Disciples of Christ, and the faith of the Holy Scriptures.

"If ye continue in my words, then are ye my disciples indeed: and ye shall know the truth, and the truth shall make you free." John 8:31,32

Commentary: The Disciples of Christ are those people who study and learn the teachings of Jesus, and practice them in their own lives. By continuous practice of Christ teachings, we will learn the truth, for truth is that which corresponds to facts. These facts about the Christian faith are revealed by the Holy Spirit, who himself is truth (read I John 5:6 and St. John 14:17 & 26).

There are many people who's hearts are covered by the veil of ignorance, others by rebellion, egotistic and are captives of their own self pride and doing. Once these people study the teachings of Christ and accept them, they will then practice the truth and hold it fast to their hearts, and then it will lift the veil and make them free. By grace are they saved.

Can we close our eyes and ears to the truth and remain innocent before God?

Bible Reference: *"He that turneth away his ears from hearing the law, even his prayer shall be abomination."* Proverbs 28:9

Commentary: There are many types of Christians. There are those who turn from the law, yet pray and do other works for the Lord, then there are those who live by the law. Both are careful and religious people. The one who turns from the law does not acknowledge the divine law as a guide for righteous living. What does that tell us? That there are many who are willing to serve God, but only if they can do it their way, they do not seek the will of God, only their own. In doing it their way, error and wrong interpretation is the result, and the Christian church becomes split more than it has already.

This is the work of egotistic people. The Bible, the whole book is holy and all must be accepted or none of it. It is God's will that we should accept the whole of God's law. (See St. John 14:15 and 15:10 and Romans 8:3,4). It is the stain of sin that comes between God and man.

"But your iniquities (sins) have separated between you and your God, and your sins have hid his face from you, that he will not hear." Isaiah 59:2

We must keep the spirit of the law and obey and practice the letter of the law or our prayers will become an abomination. To do would sanction willful rebellion.

(2:19) Christ talks about doctrine.

"If any man will do his will, he shall know of the doctrine, whether it be of God, or whether I speak of myself." John 7:17

Commentary: He who sincerely seeks true enlightenment and desires to do the will of God, will receive his needs and be able to evaluate correctly the doctrine of others. God will give illumination to those whom he knows will follow in the light of what has been revealed.

"The meek will he guide in judgment: and the meek will he teach his way." Psalms 25:9 (read St. John 8:12)

(2:20) God with holds his grace from those who reject truth?

"Because they received not the love of the truth, that they might be saved. And for this cause God shall send them strong delusion, that they should believe a lie: that they might be dammned who believed not the truth, but had pleasure in unrighteousness." II Thessalonians 2:10-12

Commentary: St. Paul writes the underlying cause or the reason why unbelievers are deceived. They had the opportunity to receive the truth and hold it fast and love the truth. But through the power of free choice, they gave up that privilege. They not only rejected the truth but also refused to seek the truth. The final condemnation of sinners will be based on their rejection of Jesus, who is the truth. A notation should be made on strong delusion. It literally means "A working of error" (see verse 9). Which lead to the final error that results in condemnation. The lie which St. Paul writes is the great deception when Satan impersonates Christ. There can be no worse lie than this.

(2:21) Fate that awaits blind teachers and their followers

"Let them alone: they be blind leaders of the blind. And if the blind lead the blind, both shall fall in the ditch." Matthew 15:14

Commentary: The meaning of this verse is that a blind teacher will only end up leading you into error.

(2:22) Gates of the Heavenly City.

"Open ye the gates, that the righteous nation which keepeth the truth may enter in." Isaiah 26:2

Commentary: New Jerusalem (Rev. 21:2) will be called the city of the righteous, the faithful city. (See Isaiah 1:26). Only those Christian who accept Christ as their Saviour and practice his teaching and love the truth will enter the gates of New Jerusalem (Rev. 22:14 and St. Matthew 7:21-27).

The Third Order of Divinity

"The Act of Holy Prayer"

I John Paul, Servant of Christ Jesus, by the grace of God, write this commentary on The *Act of Holy Prayer.* My blessings I send you. Peace from God our Father and from our Lord and Saviour Jesus of Nazareth called the Christ. Prayer is a spiritual exercise by which we are able to obtain help, knowledge, understanding, blessings and graces, counseling, inspirations, and divine revelation. Prayer is the means by which we can receive the Lord's holy blessings and the spiritual gifts of the Holy Spirit. Prayer is a daily devotion that must be exercised if we are to communicate with our Creator, to talk to and share our love, to exchange and express thoughts, to spiritually experience a union, a oneness with God.

For those people who seek to obtain one of God's spiritual gifts, to them, prayer and contemplation is a way of spiritual transformation, by which all holy men, prophets, priests, rabbis, teachers, and healers should experience. It prepares us and conditions us in a way that is acceptable to God.

Prayer is not reciting old or new words or offering just song and praises. It is a state of being, a correct frame of mind, one enters into in order to talk and experience God. When we pray we begin by closing our eyes and concentrate on our breathing, inhaling the divine breath of life, the spirit of God, through our nose.

"And the Lord formed man of the dust of the ground, and breathed into his nostrils the breath of life…" Genesis 2:7

Commentary: Exhale out through our mouth. In doing this first we are than able to release all of the day's stress and tension thereby causing our body to relax and our mind to become more calm and receptive. When we concentrate on our breathing, remember it's the breath of life. Visualize (picture) the divine breath as a white, pure, and energizing light entering your body. Feel it strengthen and renew you, as you fill up your stomach, then feel it remove all bad energy and negative feelings as you exhale. By continuing this method you will become totally relaxed.

Once you become relaxed, your mind will become calm and your brain wave levels will become lower, at a level of consciousness which is the proper state of being for divine prayer. In this state of being our consciousness becomes open, receptive, and ready to receive divine inspiration or send up proper prayer.

The Holy Spirit will guide us into the proper frame of thought, and help us use the correct words in our prayer, in accordance with our needs. In this state of prayer our consciousness is able to concentrate and focus our attention upon a single point of thought or action. Thereby increasing our ability to open up the proper channel of communication between you and God. Because we are all of the one and same divine spiritual essence, we can, through holy prayer, communicate with all forms of life created by God. Each able to transmit and receive thought, expressions, or vibrations, each according to its created ability.

Divine prayer is not a new method of prayer, but a clearer understanding of what true prayer should be. We should never beg for anything, but ask, never communicate in a form that belittles your creative abilities, but respectfully humble yourself before the Lord your God. When you pray to your Father in heaven, tell him of your joy and happiness, not only your sins and problems, then say unto the Lord "*Let it be according to thy will,"* then give thanks to him for hearing your prayer. All prayers should end in the Lords most holy name, *"In Jesus name I pray,"* Amen. This is according to the Holy Scriptures.

"And whatsoever ye shall ask in my name, that will I do, that the father may be glorified in the Son. If ye shall ask any thing in my name, I will do it." John 14:13,14

When you thank God for his help you say it in a manner as if it was already done, solved, and corrected. In doing this you have established faith in God accepted the truth that he has heard your prayer and answered them. This is the act of divine prayer, which is a very moving spiritual experience. Remember, when you pray it should always be *"Thy will be done."*

When our prayers are not answered, our problems are not solved, and have not obtained healing it is not because our heavenly Father has not heard us, or because we are too sinful and not worthy to receive an answer. Always look to understand why God did not answer your prayer, or try to understand the purpose for doing so. It could be a lesson for you to learn, or a test of your love, or part of your spiritual growth, or for you to be a witness unto the Lord. Whatever the reason, look for enlightenment and don't wallow in your own self-pity. God still loves you, and when the time is right, his blessing will come upon you. Often, in times when we show signs of first helping ourselves that the blessing of God is poured out.

The Importance of Prayer:

(3:1) Does God hear our prayers? Does he answer prayers? The Holy Scriptures gives us the answer to these questions and more.

"O thou that hearest prayers, unto thee shall all flesh come." Psalms 65:2

Commentary: God hearest all prayers, when we pray we use divine thoughts and words, which describes faith, hope, and endurance. We come to him with readiness of mind, and a gentle heart, open to receiving his understanding. Through grace by our faith in Christ Jesus as our savior and Lord, our immortal soul stands right before God. To obtain an answer to your prayer you must be right with God in heart and mind.

(3:2) God will reward.

"But without faith it is impossible to please him for he that cometh to God must believe that he is, and that he is a rewarder of them that diligently seek him." Hebrews 11:6

Commentary: In order for one to have open communication with God, one must first believe in his existence, thereby having faith in him. We are all finite creatures, and there will be times that we must have faith in something or someone whom we cannot see nor touch. Yet, if we accept the Biblical teaching accordingly, the greatest exercise of all is divine prayer, which can be exalted and carry authority by using God's words. Divine prayer is a form of positive statement, condition of character and personality. Through divine prayer, God will mold our character, as a workman ready for his labor.

Once we have established our faith in God, we begin to seek him through various spiritual exercises of prayer and meditation. When we seek him with an open heart, that is when we will find him in the state of love.

(3:3) God blesses those who pray to him.

"If ye then, being evil, know how to give good gifts unto your children, how much more shall your Father which is in heaven give good things to them that ask him?" Matthew 7:11

Commentary: If a man who robs and kills can still find time to buy a gift for a little girl in his state of sinfulness. God, who is divine, loving, and righteous, how more is God willing to give you his blessings and graces.

(3:4) God's willingness.

"He that spared not his own Son, but delivered him up for us all, how shall he not with him also freely give us all things? Romans 8:32

Commentary: If God delivered up his only begotten Son for the salvation of man, how can he then not provide for us the things we need for life and other blessings. Man's salvation is given freely by God through grace in faith in Jesus Christ.

The First Step in Prayer

(3:5) How shall we pray?

"Ask, and it shall be given you; seek and ye shall find; knock, and it shall be opened unto you: For every one that asketh receiveth; and he that seeketh findeth; and to him that knocketh it shall be opened." Matthew 7:7,8

Commentary: We should take it on faith that God is, and that what we ask for will be provided, but only if there is a true need and purpose for having it. God gives us what we need and not what we desire.

(3:6) Perfect gifts from God.

"Every good gifts and every perfect gift is from above, and cometh down from the Father of lights…" James 1:17

Commentary: God is the source of all moral, natural, supernatural, mental, and physical benefits. These good gifts falls upon all people, *Christian and non-Christian. One of the divine nature is the act of giving. "…let him ask of God, that giveth to all men liberally,…" St. James 1:5 and only good gifts come from God, they are perfect to the point where all evil elements are excluded.*

(3:7) *Ask God.*

"If any of you lack wisdom, let him ask of God…" James 1:5

Commentary: St. James realized that his new converts did not yet have the full faith and understanding of how to live a Christian life. Wisdom goes beyond understanding because knowledge alone cannot guarantee that you will take the right action on life problems. From spiritual guidance, we receive wisdom, which then helps us place a proper value upon everything in life and ensure us of the use of this knowledge. We ask God for wisdom but it is up to us to make the right decision. Life is making right choices.

Conditions to Answered Prayers

(3:8) How do we ask God?

"But let him ask in faith, nothing wavering… For let not that man think that he shall receive anything of the Lord." James 1:6,7

Commentary: When we pray to God for help we step out in faith that he will answer our request. Divine prayer mean believing that action is the forerunner for having our needs fulfilled. For prayer without any trusting faith is useless. We are not only to turn to the true source of all good blessing, we are to have a spiritual experience entering into conscious union with the Lord, believing in his ability and willingness to help. Many times man does not receive the blessing he seeks because his trust in God's is wavering, having doubts about God is a improper thought and should not be allowed to enter your mind in times of Holy Prayer.

(3:9) God's turns away.

"If I regard iniquity in my heart, the Lord will not hear me." Psalms 66:18

Commentary: In Holy Prayer, we must come before God, having no knowledge of sin in our hearts. We must be humble, sincere, and trusting in order for our prayers to be acceptable to God. It is best to open your prayer for blessing for others first before asking God to bless us. Then ask God for forgiveness of your sins, so you may come before God with a clean heart (see St. James 4:3).

(3:10) Abominations unto God.

"He that turneth away his ear from hearing the law, even his prayer shall be abomination." Proverbs 28:9

Commentary: There are some people who love God and do good deeds, yet are misguided by false teaching, believing that the law of God has no bearing on their lives, accepting one law and not another. Some wish to serve God only if they can do it their own way. Some churches teach that we are saved by grace only and that the law was done away with. These churches fail to differentiae between God divine laws and the old sacrificial laws dealing with animal sacrifice.

"For verily I say unto you, till heaven and earth pass, one jot or one tittle shall in no wise pass from the law, till all be fulfilled." Matthew 5:18

Only true Christine will take the whole of God's law as an authoritative expression of his will. For if we are true Christians, and then out of our great love for Him, we will obey his commandments. "If ye love me, keep my commandments." John 14:15 We need to over come the desires of the flesh and walk after the spirit. *"That the righteousness of the law might be fulfilled in us, who walk not after the flesh, but after the Spirit."* Romans 8:4

Sin sets up a wall or barrier between God and you. "But your iniquities have separated between you and your God, and your sins have hid his face from you, that he will not hear." Isaiah 59:2 Brothers, never go contrary to your conscience for the Holy Spirit guides us by way of our consciousness. It is the indwelling power of the Holy Spirit that helps us keep both the letter and the spirit of the law. The law also expresses the character and inner nature of God. By obeying the law, we transform our inner being to become the same as God. Most people are rebellious at heart, not wanting to change or humble themselves.

(3:11) Christ teaches us to pray.

"But I say unto you, love your enemies, bless them that curse you, do good to them that hate you, and pray for them which despiteful use you, and persecute you." Matthew 5:44

Commentary: You can never truly pray for another if there are negative feelings or emotions stress within your heart. Your prayers must be sincerely given to God, with love for another human being. Remove all envy, hate, anger, and other negative feelings from within your being, and then offer a true, sincere, and loving prayer for your fellow man. Only then will God receive your prayer and bless you. For the love you express outward, shall return unto you. This is a strong test of Christine faith, to pray for an enemy and to forgive and love those who hurt you, curse you, and use you. This is not easy to do, but it is the way of Christ, and we, as Christians, must follow the ways of Christ.

(3:12) God's forgiveness.

"And when ye stand praying, forgive, if ye have ought against any: That your Father also which is in heaven may forgive you your trespasses." Mark 11:25

Commentary: This Scriptures expresses the eastern teachings of "Karma" which states that when you do good unto others, then good will return unto you. Now this does not mean that I accept or agree with all the teachings of Eastern Philosophy, I do believe that truth can be found in all Four Corners of the earth. When our faith and love in God grows and we practice his divine teachings of understanding, forgiveness, then our own sins shall be forgiven. For how we judge others, the same way we shall be judged. With whatever measure we used to judge other, the same measure will be used in our judgement. We should never harbor or nurturer an un-forgiving spirit. As good Christians, we should practice this divine act, for even Christ, at the moment of his death, forgave those who crucified him.

Time, Place, and Content of Prayer

(3:13) Christ taught secrete prayer.

"But thou, when thou prayest, enter into thy closet (Deep prayer and Contemplation) and when thou has shut thy door, pray to thy Father which is in secret: and thy Father which seeth in secret shall reward thee openly." Matthew 6:6

Commentary: Holy prayer is a personal experience between God and you. Then there is public prayer, which is not so personal yet just as effective. When you enter privately into prayer always remember that God knows what's in your heart and on your mind. God gives personal attention to each endeavor prayer.

(3:14) Where to pray.

"And when he had sent the multitudes away, he went up into a mountain apart to pray: and when the evening was come, he was there alone." Matthew 14:23

Commentary: Jesus went up to the hills, into the deserts, on mountainside, and into the gardens to pray. To pray to the Heavenly Father in secret. A private devotion between his Father and himself, a personal experiences. Without the multitudes around him he was able to think clearly and to meditate upon his thoughts and offer a divine prayer of love and forgiveness, to communicate with a clear conscience.

(3:15) Our prayers should be mingled with.

"Be careful for nothing; but in everything by prayer and supplication with thanksgiving let your request be made known unto God." Philippians 4:6

Commentary: When we discuss our needs with God, always remember to give thanks to him for providing everything we have and will have. Thank him in a way as if your blessing has already been received. St. Paul uses the words "nothing" so believers need not have anxiety about God's ability. For there is nothing too great or too small that God cannot help with. St. Paul also lists prayers and supplication, using the word prayer in the general sense or meaning, and supplication, as a prayer for some particular needs.

"Always in every prayer of mine for you all making request with joy" Philippians 1:4

(3:16) How often should we pray?

"Praying always with all prayer and supplication in the spirit, and watching thereunto with all perseverance and supplication for all saints." Ephesians 6:18

Commentary: We should make it a duty (desire) to pray everyday, in the morning upon rising, at noon if you have the time, and in the evening upon retiring. Pray on all occasions and throughtout all seasons, and without ceasing "Pray without ceasing." I Thessalonians 5:17 in verse eight (8) St. Paul seems to be talking about spiritual weapons of war. But prayer is not a weapon, but a manner in which the entire armour of God can be worn. Many times we know what to say in our prayers, but reveal it in a poor and sometimes ignorant way. We should thank our Lord Jesus Christ for his promise of sending the Holy Spirit. You must allow the Holy Spirit to guide you or help you in choosing the correct words to properly express your true intention in a manner that is acceptable to God. By allowing the Holy Spirit to be present, in the form of thoughts, the proper words to use in our prayer, we are praying in spirit.

(3:17) In Jesus name.

"And whatsoever ye shall ask in my name, that will I do, that the Father may be glorified in the Son." John 14:13

Commentary: By asking our heavenly Father, the things we need, in his Son's name (Jesus) we are then glorifying the Father in the Son. Jesus is telling us, directly, that when we pray, we must ask what we need in his name. And the Father, who loves his Son, will do everything possible to fulfill that prayer, provided that your needs are sincere and that you truly need them.

Holy Prayers

The Christian faith has a number of holy prayers, which were prayed by Jesus Christ, written by the apostles and the early Church fathers, under the guidance of the Holy Spirit. These prayers have been used for countless years, some hundred and others thousands of years. Let us review these Holy prayers, which many Christians Churches use. Let us learn of their value.

The Lords Prayer

"Our Father, who art in heaven, hallowed by thy name. Thy kingdom come, thy will be done, on earth as it is in heaven. Give us this day our daily bread, and forgive us of our trespasses, as we forgive those who have trespassed against us, and lead us not into temptation, but deliver us from evil." Matthew 6:9

Commentary: The Lords prayer is the must holiest prayer of all, because our Lord himself said it. During the three years of apprenticeship training that the apostles had with our Lord, they were blessed to witness, experience, and receive such enlightenment, that most people would give up everything they own, to have the opportunity to learn from Jesus himself. Jesus taught his disciples his holy prayer, and the meaning and advantage that the prayer has to offer. In the prayer that is written above what our Lord Himself said, is a prayer that contains everything we need or could ask for. After repeating it many times, we some times forget the various meanings this prayer has, and the power it carries when we use it in faith.

We at times can not see its full meaning, yet to others who are ready to receive, they can write a whole page of understanding on each word. This holy prayer is called "The Lords Prayer," because Jesus first spoke the words. It is also called the "Our Father" taken from the opening statement.

The first word of this prayer is "Our" which show or is taken to mean, that we are all brethren of the same flesh and that God is our Father, the Creator of all. So when we pray this prayer, it is not done in a single action, for ourselves alone, but for all of God's children.

The word "Father" refers to God because he is our Father. But it is not to be taken to mean Father, the first of the Blessed Trinity, but the blessed Trinity itself, as God, one God. The word Father is the chosen word, for the role of a Father is to love and care for his children, to provide what they need, to teach them the values they need to learn. He provides food, clothing, and shelter. He teaches us moral values, his actions testify that he is our Father.

Before the birth of our Lord, the Hebrew nation, when they prayed, did not even use his name or dare call him Father, because they feared him more than they loved him. When our Lord came, he taught the people to look upon God as a loving Father. He was just, kind, and merciful. The people of Israel followed God out of fear and not love, and the Christians follow God out of love. Jesus taught his disciples and all Christian to call God by the sweet name of Father.

Note: I believe in this day of age, that the Jewish people do follow God out of love as does the Christians.

It is the Christian Church teachings that God is everywhere. The statement "Who art in heaven," means that where even God is, there is heaven. So, to be with God is to be in heaven, with him. This statement is not to be taken as a limit that God can only be in one place. Remember that he is all knowing, all-powerful, and is everywhere.

The word "Hallowed" means to make holy or sacred. We hold the Bible to be Holy and Sacred, because it contains the words or thoughts of God. In the statement "The kingdom come," is a petition, asking *God to come into our hearts, for when God dwells within us, in our hearts, we have the kingdom of God here, now, within us.*

"Neither shall they say, Lo here! Or Lo there! For, behold. The kingdom of God is within you." Luke 17:21 each man may attain his eternal salvation by the grace of God.

"Thy will be done on earth as it is in heaven," this sentence is stating that, it is our desire to obey the will of our heavenly Father. It also reminds us that, Adam, our first parent, did not obey the will of our heavenly Father. The angel of heaven always obeys God's will, and Jesus through his prayer, has taught us now to desire the same.

"Give us this day our daily bread," Bread has always been a symbol of food, clothing, light, heat, and air. In other words it represents the necessary things needed to sustain life. The key word in this sentence is "daily" telling us to ask daily and teach us not to be greedy, not to ask for unnecessary things. To ask for only those things we need.

"And forgive us our trespasses," as we forgive those who trespass against us." The word trespass comes from the Hebrew "Asham" which means "Offense" and "Guilt," "unfaithfulness," and "A dereliction of duty." In another words our offense to God, is our sins, and as we forgive others who have sinned against us, so God will forgive us of our sins, which we have committed against him. If we as finite humans, can forgive others, God being infinite and divine, can do no less, because he is God being divine and righteous.

"And lead us not into temptation." We are placed, on daily bases, into a position, which we have to choose from right or wrong. The temptation means an influence from the devil to do wrong. God Himself does not lead us into temptation; we are beings, of free choice. However, he does allow us to fall into temptation, he let's others tempt us, all for our learning or to show us the results of our test of love. But we can over come any temptation by the help and grace of God. In this petition we are asking God to always bless us with his grace to overcome the temptation put on us as a test. We should always view temptation as a test. We fail only when we allow the temptation to overcome us; as a result we have sinned.

"Deliver us from evil." A great petition of salvation to protect and deliver us from all forms of sin, such as the sin of murder, the sin of stealing and the sin of adultery. The final closing of this prayer is "Amen." which means, "Be it so."

The Angelica Salutation

Hail, thou that art highly flavoured, the lord is with thee: blessed art thou amongst women." St. Luke 1:28

Commentary: It was the angel Gabriel who appeared to Mary and greeted her by saying "Hail, thou that art highly flavoured, The Lord is with thee: blessed are thou amongst women." St. Luke 1:28 These are the words used by Gabriel when he appeared to tell the blessed virgin that she was selected to become the **"Theotokos,"** the birth-giver of God or the God-bearer.

The angel Gabriel adds to his salutation an important comfort; "The Lord is with thee." Mary was highly favored by God; she became the chosen God-bearer. God loves all

His creatures and in this love, He is with all of them, but Mary held a special place in his divine plan, so He is with her in a very special manner.

The second part of this salutation was taken from St. Elizabeth greeting, Mary cousin, who said to her when she saw her "Blessed are thou amongst women and blessed is the fruit of thy womb." St. Elizabeth salutation here emphasizes the fact that Mary is blessed amongst women thus called the blessed Mary, or the Blessed Mother. Since the time of the prophecy of the coming Messiah, it was the wish of all women to be the God-bearer, and Mary was the Lord anointed.

The third and last part of the angelic salutation was made up from the Holy Church herself. "Holy Mary, Mother of God, pray for us sinners, now and at the hour of our death." Amen. In that point of history, when one person met another, the salutation was not hello, but hail, and this was the proper form of greeting. Remember, at the beginning of the Angelic salutation, the angel Gabriel greeted Mary by saying "Hail", Mary full of grace. The reason why Gabriel said "Full of Grace" is because she was God's anointed one. She is to be the Mother of His Son, most favored women among all the women of that time, because she was full of God's love. Remember that grace is a state of being, which means that she was right with God. The Angel Gabriel knew that there was no sin in Mary, she was a pure virgin, gifted with every virtue.

We know that Mary is the Mother of God, for her Son Jesus is very much a part of the most holy and divine deity. A divine being of the Holy Trinity. Every catholic prays to Mary because of their ideology of her special relationship that every mother has with their sons. The Roman Catholics pray to Mary because they believe that she is alive, living in heaven. The Orthodox Catholic revere her as being a most holy women, the "Theotokos," the God-bearer.

The Protestant churches accept Mary as just another women of the Bible. As for me, I think that Mary, at the time of her death, could have been translated into heaven body and soul, by the love Jesus has for his earthly mother, just like the patriarch Enoch, the prophet and law giver, Moses, and the prophet Elijah, remember, with God nothing is impossible. My personal thoughts on this are, if she was honored with this great blessing to become the Mother of God, then I cannot believe her son (Jesus), would allow here to die, but would translate her into heaven to be with him? This would explain the many apparitions of her that are witness today and have been witness in history past.

In the Holy Scriptures we are told to pray for one another. "Confess your faults one to another, and pray one for another…" St. James 5:16. If we can ask our family members, friends or relatives to pray for us, then why can't we ask Mary the Mother of God to pray for us if we believe that she was translated into heaven? We cannot fully understand the love that exists between Jesus and his earthly mother.

Mary does not order, she does not tell her son, she does not interfere in the divine plan that God has set before the universe. Mary knows her place as the Mother of God, and if she is now immortal, she still is not God.

The Fourth Order of Divinity

"The Lord Our God"

I John Paul, a Servant of Christ Jesus, by the grace of God, write this Biblical Commentary on the *Lord our God.* My blessings go with you, peace from God our Father and from our Lord and Saviour Jesus of Nazareth called the Christ. Philosophers, theologians, metaphysicians, religious scientist, scientist, and occult leaders have all, over the century, tried to define the power, the being, and the existence of God. In their endeavors to accomplish this, they have labeled, named and described him in this manner. According to the teachings of metaphysics, religious science, and several large occult groups and churches have used the following definition to describe God: "First Cause" "Natural Law" "Cosmic Force" "Ultimate reality" "Absolute intelligence" and Universal consciousness."

Theologians of various Christian churches, and other church leaders and elders have define God as: "God" "Lord" "Creator" "Yahweh" and "Jehovah." Have described him as being supernatural, possessing the three great divine powers "Omnipotent" which means he is all powerful "Omniscient" which means he is all wise "Omnipresent" which means he is present in all places.

The Holy Scriptures attribute the following titles and describe him as Creator, ruler, sustainer, law giver, judge, and Father (Gen. 18.25; Deut. 33:2, Psalms 103:13 and 104:27-29;Isaiah 40:28 Daniel 4:17; Acts 17:25-28; Romans 8:15). The Holy Bible in itself does not contain a definition of the name "God," yet his existence and attributes are on every page. Only two names are used in the Old Testament scriptures for the only true divine being "Elohim" commonly translated as God and Jehovah translated Lord. In man's finite language we can never truly define God. But we can learn about him from the book he himself inspired.

The evidence of God's existence is found in his creation. The knowledge and wisdom of God is found in His holy book, for God has revealed himself to us in the Holy Scriptures. Only accept the truth the Bible reveals about God. Any speculation beyond what the Bible tells us of God's creative ability, the number of times he communicated with man, and of his love. We are told he is merciful, gracious, long suffering, and abundant in goodness and truth. Many of the writings set forth in the Holy Scripture tell of the ethical nature of God.

"Who shall ascend into the hill of the Lord? Or who shall stand in his holy place? He that hath clean hands, and a pure heart; who hath not lifted up his soul unto vanity, nor sworn deceitfully. He shall receive the blessing from the Lord, and righteousness from the God of his salvation" Psalms 24:3-5

Your conception of God could never be complete until you study the character and life of Jesus. For Christ himself has said *"...He that hath seen me hath seen the Father;..."* St. John 14:9 Only Jesus is the full expression of God. In the sacrifice of Christ, we see and learn of the infinite wisdom, love, justice, and mercy of God. Through the knowledge and practice of Christ teachings will bring about a personal transformation of our own being.

The Creator and His Creation

(4:1) Heaven and Earth made.

> *"In the beginning God created the heaven and the earth."* Genesis 1:1

Commentary: The very first verse of the Holy Scriptures declares God as our Creator (Gen. 1:1). Everything in the universe has a time for its beginning and end. But God's existence is Eternal; God is without a beginning or end. Affirms that God is before all else, that he is the one and only cause of all else. Here in this verse is set forth the holy truth, that in the creation of the world. God was not in need of pre-existing matter. For at the time of creation, the existence of matter came forth in creation, and in itself was matter created. No declaration can be more fitting than to introduce God as an "Omnipotent" being. A deity possessing a personality, a will, and having a purpose, thus exercising his divine will by creating the heaven and the earth.

God in his divine form is Spirit (John 4:24), and reveal himself to express a true working knowledge of himself to those persons who, in faith, open themselves up to this divine self-revelation. The fundamental nature of God, from a biblical point of view, reveal the truth that God is unique in nature and that he is personal, spiritual, and most holy. God is the great Creator, transcendent and sovereign Lord. No one can live on his or her own power and authority, independent of divine sovereignty.

(4:2) God created the Heaven and Earth.

> *"By the word of the Lord were the heavens made; and all the host of them by the breath of his mouth"…"For he spake, and it was done; he commanded, and it stood fast."* Psalms 33:6-9

Commentary: God created all things, his works are done in truth *"For the word of the Lord is right; and all his works are done in truth."* Psalms 33:4 His words are right. God in unity with Christ (the word) created all things. Jesus is declared to be the "word" "In the beginning was the word, and the word was with God, and the word was God. The same was in the beginning with God. All things were made by him; and without him was not anything made that was made." John 1:1-3 Who took part in God's creation. In contrast with all other deities of the world, God is set forth as Creator, claiming creative ability (Genesis 1:3-26). When God spake it was done, He commanded and it stood fast. Our universe still function under divine laws and exists and has order. It stands fast.

(4:3) God creates through Jesus

"For by him were all things created that are in heaven, that are in earth, visible and invisible, whether they be thrones, or dominion's or principalities or power: all things were created by him, and for him." Colossians 1:16

Commentary: In this verse the word "Him" is referring to Christ for Jesus is the center and source from where creation originated. It's the creative power, which proves the divinity of Christ "Hath in these last days spoken unto us by his Son, whom he hath appointed heir of all things, by whom also he made the worlds." Hebrews 1:2

"Wherefore, holy brethren, partakers of the heavenly calling, consider the Apostles and high priest of our profession, Christ Jesus." Hebrews 3:1

According to this verse Jesus is the high priest in the Holy Sanctuary in heaven.

The Aaronic priesthood was instituted by Moses, under God's instruction. Christ now supersedes the earthly, Aaronic priesthood, because he is sent forth as God and as high priest. He is the heir to all of his creation, for he took off his royal robe, laid down his kingly crown, returned the royal scepter to his Father and stepped down from his throne to become incarnated into human form to pay the price the law demands of our sins. No other religion can confess that their God laid down his life for his creatures and for his creation.

Israel had been taught *"Hear, O Israel, the Lord our God is one Lord."* Deuteronomy 6:4 It was necessary for the New Testament writers to help Israel understand that the Messiah has come, and share the throne of the Father. For they both take part in creation, working together as fellow workers, with one goal, plan, and purpose in mind, creating the magnitude of the universe with un-numbered millions of worlds circling the Throne of God.

The account of creation runs parallel in the two verses of Genesis 1:1 and St. John 1:1 both with the same opening statement of divine power. *"In the beginning,"* one stating the beginning of creation (Gen.1:1) and the other stating the existence of Jesus with God, his Father, before the beginning of creation (St. John 1:1). Both verses make powerful claims that God created heaven and earth.

(4:4) God's reason for making the earth.

"For thus saith the Lord that created the heavens; God himself that formed the earth and made it; he hath established it, he created it not in vain, he formed it to be inhabited: I am the Lord; and there is none else." Isaiah 45:18

Commentary: Our world was not created in vain. It was God's design and plan that the earth became the home of the human race. Man is to inhabit the earth and make it his home, regardless how the power of sin causes man to treat the earth and his fellow creature. God's will and purpose, will be carried out to its divine end.

It is our duty to learn and know of God existence. A type of unity with God restored. A unity that Adam and Eve had with God before the great fall. This unity is not to be confuse with metaphysical unity. A Christian unity with God is a relational unity, a oneness of mind, desire and will.

(4:5) God's Power upholds all things.

"Who being the brightness of his glory, and the express image of his person, and upholding all things by the word of his power, when he had by himself purged our sins, sat down on the right hand of the Majesty on high." Hebrews 1:3

Commentary: Words are a form of communication, which expresses our thoughts. Some words are spoken with authority that can manifest our will, thereby creating physical reality. Jesus Christ, when on earth, spoke with authority and by the power of his words also manifested his will as miracles. It is Christ who upholds all things in this universe, who establishes order, natural and universal laws of nature, who keeps the heavenly bodies not only in motion, but their appointed orbits. Compare the phrase *"By him all things consist"* Colossians 1:17 meaning by Christ all things are held together.

The Holy Scriptures declares that God is "Spirit" which informs us that he is life and power (John 4:24). His spiritual nature is the true reality that God is absolute Power and Life giver. He is the invisible transcendent living power from whom all life and existence bring forth from (Acts 17:28).

(4:6) The heavens declare?

"The heavens declare the glory of God; and the firmament sheweth his handywork." Psalms 19:1

Commentary: The word heaven in this verse is what appears to us in the sky, the region which includes the Sun, Plants, and Stars (Gen.1:1-20). When one looks upon the night sky, it impresses upon the beholder a sense of the glory of God. The word firmament is translated from the Latin Vulgate *"Firmamentum"* which literally means "A Support" manifesting as a solid (physical) but firm universe, existing as a well planned and organized universe created by God, and not just happen by chance.

(4:7) Man's perception through creation.

"For the invisible things of him from the creation of the world are clearly seen, being understood by the things that are made, even his eternal power and Godhead; so that they are without excuse." Romans 1:20

Commentary: The invisible things, meaning his eternal power of creation, working in the universe unseen by men. Yet, his results are manifested and perceived clearly by those men who seek him. The abundant evidence of his goodness and love are all around us and testify and acknowledge his power of creation. St. Paul writes of his divine essence which brings to us his holy revelation, the Holy Scriptures, and his works is in nature and through man conscience and understanding is enough to enlighten men of divine works, power and invisible things, such as electricity, gravity, and magnetic fields.

The Character of God.

(4:8) God's nature?

"The Lord is righteous in all his ways, and holy in all his works." Psalms 145:17

Commentary: The Lord our God is righteous, holy, and has the mark of divinity. God is just and He will not punish sinners more than they deserve.

(4:9) Christ attributes.

"By his knowledge shall my righteous servant justify many; for he shall bear their iniquities." Isaiah 53:11

Commentary: God calls his divine, only begotten Son, righteous, the bearer of our iniquities. For Christ alone knows the character and will of the Father. He said that he has come to reveal the Father to men "All things are delivered unto me of my Father: and no man knoweth the Son, but the Father; neither knoweth any man the Father, save the Son, and he to whomsoever the Son will reveal him." Matthew 11:27 (see St. John 1:8, 5:19, 8:28, 10:15, and 17:3). He shall also bear man's sins (see verse 4-6, 8, and 10). "Because thou wilt not leave my soul in hell, neither wilt thou suffer thine holy one to see corruption." Acts 2:27 In the last commentary God declares the messiah, Jesus, the righteous servant. Here God declares him to be holy.

(4:10) The justice of God.

"He is the rock, his work is perfect: for all his ways are judgment: a God of truth and without iniquity, just and right is he." Deuteronomy 32:4

Commentary: He is perfect in his work, and never leaves anything unfinished. He is a God of truth and principles, one who acts in harmony with his own divine works. He is without sin or any kind of corruption, full of just and standing righteous. He is God.

(4:11) God's strength and wisdom.

"Behold, God is mighty, and despiseth not any: he is mighty in strength and wisdom." Job 36:5

Commentary: This is clear, He is mighty in strength and in wisdom.

God exercised a force, through the power of his word that was greater than the universe, when it was at its maximum moment and brought it into existence.

(4:12) Treasures found in Christ?

"In whom are hid all the treasures of wisdom and knowledge." Colossians 2:3

Commentary: Within Christ is stored away the secrets and mystery of God. He is the Son of God and the son of man. The perfect bridge between God and man. He is a well from which all blessings spring forth. He is the treasure house of divine wisdom and knowledge. (I Cor. 1:22, 24 and Ephesians 3:9-11).

(4:13) God's faithful promises.

"Know therefor that the Lord thy God, he is God, the faithful God, which keepeth covenant and mercy with them that love him and keep his commandments to a thousand generations." Deuteronomy 7:9

Commentary: A positive statement, he is God. Faithful in keeping his promises covenant, with you. If you love and keep his commandment, he will fulfill his end of the agreement, unto a thousand generations. (20,000 years).

(4:14) God's character.

"He that loveth not knoweth not God; for God is love." I John 4:8

Commentary: Any Christian who claims to understand and know God, but does not love his fellow man, is fooling himself, because in truth he does not know God. The very essence of God's nature is love. His act of intervention in human history is nothing but love.

(4:15) God's tender compassion.

"But thou, O Lord, art a God full of compassion, and gracious, long suffering, and plenteous in mercy and truth." Psalms 86:15

Commentary: The divine nature of God is love, being compassionate, gracious, having mercy, and enduring long-suffering.

Love: The divine nature of love is that love accepts all and loves all.

Compassion*:* To love is to respect the needs and feelings of others.

Gracious: To love is to give graciously, without requirements of obligations of any kind, but is given freely.

Mercy: To love is to have mercy in your heart for those who use you and hurt you, for from mercy comes forgiveness.

Long suffering: To love is to suffer the pain of love, and to accept the pain whenever it comes. The pain of insults, the pain of betrayal, the pain of miss understanding, the pain of un-forgiveness.

The Love of God

(4:16) God Divine nature is.

"And we have known and believed the love that God hath to us. God is love; and he that dwelleth in love dwelleth in God, and God in him." 1 John 4:16

Commentary: Love is within the very essence of God's most inner nature. He proved this by allowing Jesus to give up his life as an act of love. The only religion where God, through some mystical working, came down to earth and allowed a part of his divine nature to suffer the act of human death, for the fulfillment of the covenant between God and Adam and the covenant between God and Abraham.

It is not easy to express in words of the depth of God's love; through the act so described "For God so loved the word, that he gave his only begotten son, that whosoever believeth in him should not perish, but have everlasting life." John 3:16

(4:17) God delights.

"He retaineth not his anger for ever, because he delighteth in mercy." Micah 7:18

Commentary: God becomes angered as any father would at a son who does wrong, for he is a God of deep emotion, of feelings, of love, but yet, he delights in mercy. Another divine character is the act of forgiveness and the willingness to forget. This is something that is not offended practiced among the race of men.

(4:18) God bestow his blessings.

"That ye may be the children of your Father which is in heaven: for he maketh his sun to rise on the evil and on the good, and sendeth rain on the just and on the unjust." Matthews 5:45

Commentary: Children always resemble their father in character. If we are to be called sons or children of God we must take upon us his divine nature, such as: love, compassion, mercy, and forgiveness. The test of our love for

God is our love for our fellow man "If a man say, I love God, and hateth his brother, he is a liar: for he that loveth not his brother whom he hath seen, how can he love God whom he hath not seen? 1 John 4:20 It was the old Jewish belief that God only blesses the righteous and punishes the sinners. Jesus corrected this error, and explained that our Father in heaven gives life and blessing to the righteous and give life and forgiveness to the sinners. Because both are his children, he loves them both. He does not approve of the sinful acts people do. But this does not mean that he does not love them.

Another way to know God's love is to be faithful and obedient to God teachings, laws, and principles involving our life, our relationship to our spouse, our family and relatives, and to our fellow man. To be obedient to his rules of worship, to follow his foot step in being compassionate, forgiving, and to love all things in nature that is good.

By imitating God's character of love, compassion, forgiveness, and we can come to know God.

(4:19) God's love bring us?

"Behold, what manner of love the Father hath bestowed upon us, that we should be called the sons of God: Therefore the world knoweth us not, because it knew him not." 1 John 3:1

Commentary: St. John is so overcome as he contemplated the height, depth, and magnitude of the divine affection and love of God. As it filled John's heart, so should it fill all Christian hearts. God has given us his love and nothing can alter this fact. Of all the religions of the world, no other deity has expressed his love for mankind than the God of the Christian faith. We as sinners are called by God to give up the sinful practices of the world, to accept the blood of his son as our Saviour and become his newly, chosen children, that shall inherit "The Kingdom of Heaven."

(4:20) We are the sons of God.

"For as many as are led by the spirit of God, they are the sons of God… The spirit itself beareth witness with our spirit, that we are the children of God." Romans 8:14-16

Commentary: The influence or guidance of the Holy Spirit is not a spontaneous or momentary impulse. It is a steady, increasing flow of continuous action through habitual influence. A spiritual transformation is done by leading us, by our own free choice, and will never force us. God calls us his children only if we allow ourselves to be led by the Holy Spirit, which allows us to understand the deep secrets of divine power, wisdom, and knowledge.

(4:21) the Divine love of God.

"…Because the love of God is shed abroad in our hearts by the Holy Spirit which is given unto us." Romans 5:5

Commentary: It is God's unchanging love for us which gives us assurance and hope as Christians. In turn this love leads us to love God and place upon us a sense of caring for our fellow man. This experience strengthens our love with confidence and hope. The blessing of God, through the Holy Spirit, is poured out in richness and in abundance. The Holy Spirit pours out the love of God upon our hearts and witnesses the love of Jesus (St. John 15:26 and 16:14).

As we study the Holy Scriptures, we behold the glory, perfection, and love of Jesus. We ourselves will undergo a spiritual change and become Christ-like through the influence of the spirit. "But we all, with open face beholding as in a glass the glory of the Lord, are changed into the same image from glory to glory even as by the Spirit of the Lord." II Cor. 3:18

(4:22) Appreciate God's love.

"How excellent is thy loving kindness O God! Therefor the children of men put their trust under the shadow of thy wings." Psalms 36:7

Commentary: Once we feel the presence of the Holy Spirit and know of God's love for us and experience, within us, a changing heart, we put our full trust under his care.

(4:23) The love of God.

"...The Lord thy God turned the curse into a blessing unto thee, because the Lord thy God loved thee." Deuteronomy 23:5

Commentary: The love of God for us is a shield of protection, which is able to turn anyone's curse, against you, into a blessing. All because God loves you, and is upon you.

(4:24) God show us his love.

"...My son, despise not thou the chastening of the Lord, nor faint when thou art rebuked of him... For whom the Lord loveth he chasteneth, and scourgeth every man whom he receiveth." Hebrew 12:5-6

Commentary: It would be best that I first define the meaning of some of the key words.

Despise*:* From the Greek "*Oligoreo*" means "To think lightly of" failure to take it seriously. We as children of God must take the teaching and instruction of our heavenly Father seriously. The purpose of discipline is to make an impression, so we may learn from our mistakes.

Chastening: From the Greek "Paideia" means up bringing, training, instruction, discipline and correction. "And, ye father, provoke not your children to wrath: but bring them up in the nurture and admonition of the Lord." Ephesians 6:4 To discipline a child is to train him, to correct, mold and strengthen his character. Many times the word is define or taken as a punishment or chastisement. The fine art of discipline is used in the making of excellent students and disciples, and a good disciple always submits his will to the discipline or training of the Lord.

Faint: From the Greek "Ekluo" which means to become weary, to give out, to lose courage. A disciples who always loses courage will never graduate from the school of experience. All who lose courage and give up should turn to Jesus. God is our Father in heaven, who loves us, and prepares us for our daily lesson of life. Other find that it's not the discipline, but our attitudes and rebellious hearts which makes life difficult.

Rebuked: From the Greek "Elecgcho" which means, to reprove, to correct, to punish, and to discipline. It is never easy or pleasant to accept correction, or to be reproved of our action and life style. It is natural for us to despise it or to rebel against it, yet this does not make it right. The easiest way to accept correction is to humble yourself before it. With a proper attitude will result in profit.

(4:25) Enduring God's love.

"Yea, I have loved thee with an everlasting love: Therefore with loving kindness have I drawn thee." Jeremiah 31:3

Commentary: The prophet Jeremiah declares that God's love is everlasting, and by this love, we will be forever drawn to him.

(4:26) We can not be separated from God love.

"For I am persuaded, that neither death, nor life, nor angels, nor principalities, nor powers, nor things, nor things to come, nor height, nor depth, nor any other creature, shall be able to separate us from the love of God, which is in Christ Jesus our Lord." Romans 8:38-39

Commentary: St. Paul is convinced that no power on earth or in heaven, throughout all eternity, can ever separate us from his divine love. Only through the power of free choice can the believer become separated. However, through your power of free choice, you cannot become separated as long as there exist love between God and you. Those who choose to separate themselves from God's love are lost (Colossians 1:23 and I Cor. 9:27). Even death cannot separate us from Christ's love against our will. No power of the angels (good or evil) can influence or alienate our minds to leave the love of God and his blessing.

Scholars Personal Note: On the day of creation, God set in motion universal forces which acts in accordance to billions of divine laws. These laws are in force today, and respond to our actions of disobedient with a universal reaction.

Example #1: If we touch a hot stove, universal law states that we will burn our fingers.

Example #2: If we disobey God's law on health, we will then live a life of poor health. We will live a life of pain and suffering.

Remember, all bad things that happens to us is not by the will of God, but is the result of our own action of disobedient against universal laws.

Example #3: If we say or do bad things against others, that same universal energy will fall upon us and do the same to us, but in three folds. Whenever we step outside the boundaries of God's laws, we suffer and experience the associated results.

Divine Attributes to God

(4:27) God is beyond our understanding.

"Before the mountains were brought forth, or even thou hadst formed the earth and the world, even from everlasting to everlasting, thou art God. "
Ps. 90:2

Commentary: God exists first before all creation and neither the earth or the highest heaven can contain him (I Kings 8:27). God exists in his own infinite realm of realty as the transcendent Lord over all creation existing beyond time and space. The Spirit of God differs from all other forms of spirit because his intellectual capabilities are unlimited.
(4:28) God is all knowing *"Omniscient"*

"For if our heart condemn us, God is greater than our heart, and knoweth all things. " (I John 3:20).

Commentary: God knows all inward human thoughts and outward human acts (Ps. 139). Nothing in all creation is hidden from the God's sight. Everything, every thought, words, and act is laid uncover before God presents and we all must make account for them (Hebrew 4:13).

(4:29) God is all Powerful *"Omnipotent"*

"And he said Ab'-ba, Father, all things are possible unto thee.... "
(Mark 14:36)

"For with God nothing shall be impossible. " (Luke 1:37)

Commentary: God is all Powerful and can exercise his will without any limitation. What is interesting is that God will not do anything that will be contrary to his divine nature of wisdom, love, and holiness. God cannot deny himself and always uses the intermediate angelic and human agents to carry out his will within our earthly realm. God energy is unlimited, untiring, and inexhaustible.

The Fifth Order of Divinity

"The Deity of Christ"

I John Paul, a Servant of Christ Jesus, by the grace of God, write this commentary on the *deity of Christ.* My blessings go with you, peace from God our Father and from our Lord and Saviour Jesus of Nazareth called the Christ. The Holy Scriptures of the New Testament and of the Old Testament contain the living word of God, the word is alive, because our Saviour Jesus Christ is alive, as Jesus lives, we also live. The name of Jesus comes from the Greek *"Iesous"* and from the Hebrew *"Yeshua"* taken from *Joshua"* and *Yahweh"* means salvation. Jesus is a most common name often given to young Jewish boys. It expresses the young boy's parent's faith in God and their hopes in the promise of the coming Messiah, the salvation of Israel.

The whole objective of the Holy Scriptures is to reveal to the world the existence of God, and his plans for the salvation of all mankind. It is very true that the Scriptures contain history, prophecy, laws, poetry, and drama.. It is given for our learning that we may become wise.

Who is Jesus Christ on whom every date in history hinges? To those who accept him as the Messiah, to them he is their Saviour, the Christ, the anointed. Sent by God as the salvation of the world. He is the *"Emmanuel"* God with us, Isaiah 7:14, in recognition of his deity and the virgin birth. St. Matthew 1:23

In our search to understand the message of Christ, the power and authority even his mission, we must go to the New Testament and read what he himself says and declares. As we listen to his stories, declarations and answers to the questions that were put to him. We can only say that never in the history of mankind was there such a man.

Fifteen Facts about Jesus

(5:1) He is God.

"I and my Father are One" John 10:30

Commentary: Jesus here declares his unity with the Father. One in will, one in purpose, one action, one in divine substance. The Father supports the authority of his Son. When Jesus talks about his relationship with his Father and about his divinity. The Jews of his time understood the claims of divinity that Jesus declared (St. John 5:18-19, and 10: 32-33).

(5:2) He pre-existed.

"Your father Abraham rejoiced to see my day: and he saw it and was glad… Jesus said unto them, verily, verily, I say unto you, before Abraham was, I am." John 8:56, 58

Commentary: Jesus declares of his existence long before the existence of Abraham. The expression of "I am" makes claims to his divinity. The same "I am" that God said to Moses, on Mt. Sinai. The word "I am" is the sign which Jesus uses to connect himself with the God of the Old Testament. The use of the name "Father" also connects him with the God of the Old Testament, and brings God closer to the people of Israel by referring to God as Father.

(5:3) He is the Messiah.

"…Again the high priest asked him, and said unto him, art thou the Christ, the Son of the blessed? And Jesus said, I am: and ye shall

see the son of man sitting on the right hand of power, and, coming in the clouds of heaven." Mark 14: 61-62

Commentary: Jesus again openly confesses that powerful and positive statement of his deity "I am" and associates it with the only living God *"Yahweh"* or *"Jehovah."* He shall sit at the right hand of power of God. For only the anointed Messiah is to inherit such a glory. The old Jewish leader could not accept the fact that a carpenter could be the Messiah. Yet they forgot that David was a shepherd. Is God not allowed to choose who shall be the Messiah?

(5:4) He is all-powerful.

"And Jesus came and spake unto them, saying, all power is given unto me in heaven and in earth." Matthew 28:18

Commentary: The word power comes from the Greek *"Exousia"* means *"Authority"* all authority is given unto him (St. Matthew 10:1 and St. Mark 2:10). Throughout his ministry Jesus exercised his authority (St. Matthew 7:29 and 21:23). The only deity in the world that teaches the doctrine of a deity was Jesus, who came to earth and clothes his divinity with humanity to support the principle teaching of Christianity.

(5:5) He is infallible.

"Heaven and earth shall pass away, but my words shall not pass away." Matthew 24:35

Commentary: Christ here states that the heaven (atmospheric) and earth (the planet) will long undergo fundamental changes before his divine words will ever fade. The authority, truth and principles of God's words are steadfast forever. For we all know that God changes not *"For I am the Lord, I change not;* Malachi 3:6

(5:6) He is the way and the truth.

"Jesus saith unto him, I am the way, the truth, and the life: no man cometh unto the Father, but by me." John 14:6

Commentary: Once again we hear Christ's famous expression *"I am."* He is the ladder, which goes from the earth and touches heaven. Within him exist both humanity and divinity, making him the bridge that leads us to truth, life, and to our Heavenly Father.

(5:7) He is the resurrection and the life.

"Jesus said unto her, I am the resurrection, and the life: he that believeth in me, though he were dead, yet shall he live: and whosoever liveth and believeth in me shall never die." John 11:25-26

Commentary: One of the signs of divinity is the power to resurrect a person from the dead. Christ so declared to have such power. Believing in him we have the promises of the original life, in the Garden of Eden. He has such powers. Receive him and you receive life. *"And this is the record, that God hath given to us eternal life, and this life is in his Son. He that hath the Son hath life; and he that hath not the Son of God hath not life."* 1 John 5:11-12 The assurance of a future resurrection to eternal life.

(5:8) He is the only door to salvation.

"I am the door; by me if any man enter in, he shall be saved, and shall go in and out, and find pasture." John 10:7-9

Commentary: This verse brings forth a universal call to all of mankind. Anyone can be saved who accepts Christ, who is the door. Christ declares himself as the door of salvation for in him we may all enjoy the privileges of salvation.

(5:9) He is the living bread.

"I am the living bread, which came down from heaven: if any man eat of this bread, he shall live for ever: and the bread that I will give is my flesh, which I will give for the life of the world." John 6:51

Commentary: As manna came down from heaven and fed the Hebrew nation. Christ came from heaven also, to be incarnated into the flesh to save the world. He becomes the bread, which we symbolically accept and eat during the Divine Liturgy (church service), partaking of the Lord Supper (Holy Communion), and becoming saved through constant union with our Saviour.

(5:10) He is the light of the world.

"Then spake Jesus again unto them, saying, I am the light of the world: he that followeth me shall not walk in darkness, but shall have the light of life." St. John 8:12

Commentary: Christ understood the Holy Scripture and he himself declares to be that illuminating light of life. Jesus is that lighted source by which we can all follow into eternal life. Christ sets the truth into the light, that all may read and understand.

(5:11) He is without sin.

"Which of you convinceth me of sin? And if I say the truth, why do ye not believe me." John 8:46

Commentary: The word convinceth, must be made clear for understanding. It means *"To convict,"* or *"To reprove,"* Jesus himself, through his words, his life, and his action gives testimony of his sinless life, and of his desire to conform to the Father's will. The Jewish leader knew of this, yet did not believe. So Jesus appealed to their knowledge of the matter. Their silence on the subject confirmed his testimony.

(5:12) He is omnipresence.

"Teaching them to observe all things whatsoever I have commanded you: and lo, I am with you always even unto the end of the world." Matthews 28:20

Commentary: Through the gift of the Holy Spirit, Christ is able to have fellowship with every believer, anywhere, at any time (St. John 16:7). Because he departed bodily, and went to heaven. This does not mean that he is unable to be with us in spirit and in mind.

(5:13) He has the power of prophecy.

"Now I tell you before it come, that when it is come to pass, ye may believe that I am he." John 13:19

Commentary: When you read the entire content of this chapter, you will see Jesus is foretelling of Judas defection, before it came to pass. So we may know that he has the power to foresee the future *"…Verily, Verily, I say unto you, that one of you shall betray me."* St. John 13:21

(5:14) He has the power to forgive sins.

"Jesus seeing their faith said unto the sick of the palsy; son be of good cheer; thy sins be forgiven thee." Matthew 9:2

Commentary: Jesus here exercises his authority to forgive sins, a true sign of divinity. When Jesus was questioned about his act of forgiving sins, Jesus ask the following question *"For whether is easier, to say, thy sins be forgiven thee; or to say, arise, and walk."* St. Matthew 9:35 and when they gave no answer, he told the sick man *"…take up thy bed, and go unto thine house. And* *he arose, and departed to his house."* Verse 6 and 7. As Jesus has authority over sickness, he also has authority over sins, which is also a sickness, of the Soul.

(5:15) He knows the minds and hearts of all men.

"But Jesus did not commit himself unto them, because he knew all men, and needed not that any should testify of man; for he knew what was in man." John 2:24-25

Commentary: Jesus knew the hearts of men who seek him. He often read their thoughts, thereby providing them with evidence that divinity was in him "And immediately when Jesus perceived in his spirit that they so reasoned within themselves, he said unto them, why reason ye these things in your hearts." Mark 2:8 Jesus knew before hand the events which were about to take place, and he fulfilled the prophecy of the Old Scriptures.

The Deity of Christ

(5:16) Jesus, a member of the Godhead

"But unto the son he saith, thy throne, O God, is for ever and ever…" Hebrew 1:8

Commentary: The heavenly Father here is addressing his Son, calling him God. There can be no greater testimony of the Deity of Christ than his our heavenly father declaring the son as God. From the highest authority, God declares his Son, Jesus Christ, a member of the Godhead.

(5:17) He was recognized by the Father while on earth?

"And lo, a voice from heaven, saying, this is my beloved Son, in whom I am well pleased." Matthew 3:17

Commentary: Through his entire life here on earth, the heavenly Father's voice was heard on three different occasion. 1 at his baptism, and 2. At the transfiguration, and 3. When he left the temple for the last time (see at. Matthew 17:5 and II Peter 1:16-18 and St. John 12:28).

(5:18) Christ talks about eternity

"And now, O Father, glorify thou me with thine own self with the glory which I had with thee before the world was." John 17:5

Commentary: Jesus openly prays for his former glory, which he had before his incarnation. This statement is self-evidence of Christ's pre-existence. That he truly did exist before the creation of the world.

"But thou, Bethlehem Ephratah, thou be little among the thousands of Judah yet out of thee shall he come forth unto me that is to be ruler in Israel; whose goings forth have been from of old, from everlasting." Micah 5:2

Commentary: The prophet Micah clearly states the pre-existence of the Messiah, the anointed. He, who is to come, shall be born in Bethlehem. This decree has been set forth from the days of eternity.

(5:19) Between the Father and Son?

"I and my Father are one." John 10:30

Commentary: Jesus declares his unity with the Father. The Father is behind every word and action of the Son. Both are in unity with the same will, purpose, and objectives. As declared by the early church fathers in the "Nicene" creed, both of the same substance.

(5:20) Father and Son declare?

"I am the first, and I am the last, and beside me there is no God." Isaiah 44:6

"I am alpha and omega, the beginning and the end, the first and the last." Rev. 22:13

Commentary: Both declare equal unity and eternity as one divine purpose. All of creation owes their existence to both authorities. Both existed before the universe was created and all things must end in relationship to both.

(5:21) Fullness dwells in Christ?

"For in him dwelleth all fullness of the Godhead bodily." Colossians 2:9

Commentary: Upon the character of Christ and within his very essence dwells the sum total of the divine nature of God the Father. All power, authority and responsibility of a deity reside continually upon Christ. A clear understanding of the word *"fullness"* in this verse cannot be limited to time or space nor powers. For God's quality of divinity, authority, dignity, love, perfection and divine power rest in Christ, for they are one.

The Sixth Order of Divinity

"The Holy Spirit"

I John Paul, a Servant of Christ Jesus, by the grace of God, write this commentary on the *Holy Spirit.* My blessings go with you, peace from God our Father and from our Lord and Saviour Jesus of Nazareth called the Christ. There has been much speculation on the mysterious nature, existence and works of the Holy Spirit. The performance of the Holy Spirit as a member of the deity is very interesting, for the Holy Spirit searches, knows, intercedes, helps, guides, and convicts us. The Holy Scriptures also gives us information concerning the actions of the Holy Spirit, which imply that the Holy Spirit is a person who possess a personality. The chosen writes of the Old Testament characterized him as a vitalizing, stimulating, and life sustaining being, an enabling force of divine nature which identified with God.

From the Hebrew "*"Ruach Qodesh"* and the Greek *"Hagion Pneuma"* it was usually translated in the King James Version as Holy Ghost. Except in the following verses St. Luke 11:13 and Ephesians 1:13 and 4:30 and I Thess. 4:8 where it is translated as Holy Spirit. He is the third person of the Godhead or Trinity. The prophets, apostles and other authors of the Bible experience a special relationship with the Holy Spirit. For the Bible *says,* ***"The Spirit of the Lord came upon me"*** II Chronicles 15:1; 20:14. As many of the holy people of the Bible said *"I am filled with the Holy Spirit."*

On his last night Jesus made the promise of sending to his disciples a comforter. The comforter was to carry on the works of Christ. Upon Jesus ascension, the Holy Spirit became the divinely appointed representative of Christ here on earth. The Holy Spirit has become our link between man and Christ, a comforter (St. John 14:16). Let us begin our study about the Holy Spirit as the comforter.

The Holy Spirit

(6:1) Jesus promise to his disciples.

"And I will pray the Father, and he shall give you another comforter, that he may abide with you forever." John 14:16

Commentary: Jesus knew he was going to leave his disciples, because he had work to do in heaven as the high priest. He prayed to his Father to send down a comforter, one just like him who would stay forever as a witness. From the Greek *"Parakletos,"* a word used in the New Testament only by St. John. We have *"Para"* meaning beyond and then the adjective *"Kletos,"* meaning "one called from the beyond." However, in scripture the usage of this word seems to project more of an involved sense such as is found in *"Parakaleo"* meaning "to exhort" or "to comfort."

In other pre-Christian and non-Christian writings and literature *"Parakletos"* retains a more general meaning "one who stands up on behalf of another," "a mediator," "an intercessor," "a helper," *"Blessed are they that mourn: for they shall be comforted."* St. Matthew 5:4 to call the Holy Spirit the comfort is to emphasize only one of his many features.

(6:2) The comforter.

"But the comforter, which is the Holy Spirit, whom the Father will send in my name, he shall teach you all things, and bring all things to your remembrance, whatsoever I have said unto you." John 14:26

Commentary: Much of Jesus work was healing and teaching. Upon his ascension, this task was then placed upon the Holy Spirit as on of his functions. The word *"Master"* translated from the Greek *"Didaskalos"* meaning "teacher" and it appears 41 times in the New Testament. The 12 Disciples of Christ studied and were instructed by Jesus for a period of three years. This was their seminary training. In the final year the crowning of their education was done by the Holy Spirit and upon their graduation (Pentecost), they received the blessing (laying on of hands), or being filled with the Holy Spirit and went as teachers of the Gospel and as witnesses of Christ.

In the disciples present state of mind they were unable to understand many of the teachings and truths that Jesus taught. They needed further instructions from the Holy Spirit. For only the Holy Spirit knows the things of God as it is stated "The Spirit of God knows the things of God and searcheth all things, yea, the deep things of God." I Corinthians 2:10, 11. Only those people who put aside pride and ego, and their former teachings, and humble themselves with an open heart can receive the deep understanding of the teaching relating to the things of God, imparted to them by the Holy Spirit.

Another function is to help us bring to remembrance the spiritual things we are taught. In the moments of crisis, when you are faced with the opposition in a discussion, the spirit would bring the appropriate ideas and words to mid.

(6:3) The comforter reproves the world.

"And when he is come, he will reprove the world of sin, and of righteousness, and of judgment." John 16:8

Commentary: From the Greek *"Elecgcho"* which means, "to convict." But in verse 8:46 it is translated as "reprove" (see St. Luke 3:19 and Ephesians 5:11). The Holy Spirit is to convince us of what is sin and what is righteousness. He urges us to accept the righteousness of Christ. He will correct us in our ways and bring us into understanding.

Works of the Holy Spirit

(6:4) The comforter is known.

"But when the comforter is come, whom I will send unto you from the Father, even the spirit of truth, which proceedeth from the Father, he shall testify of me." John 15:26

Commentary: The Father and the Son are one, they work in unison. Jesus sends the Holy Spirit, as the spirit of truth, in full agreement with the Father. There is no contradiction, all three personage of the Godhead hold a position and know of their oneness with each other.

(6:5) The Spirit of truth.

"...The spirit of truth, is come, he will guide you into all truth..." John 16:13

Commentary: The Holy Spirit imparts the truth to those who seek it. The truth that is referred to in this verse is primarily used in the theological sense. Even scientific inventions have always existed until, through the works of the Holy Spirit, it is rediscovered, and once understood can be used for the benefit of man. Compare the following titles bestowed upon the Holy Spirit. The spirit speaks (I Timothy 4:1), teaches (I Corinthians 2:3), bears witness (Romans 8:16), makes intercession (Romans 8:26), distributes the gifts (I Corinthians 12:11), and invites the sinner (Revelation 22:17). The Holy Spirit reveals truth in all matters of Doctrine, Prophecy and the working of nature.

(6:6) The Holy Spirit reveal.

"He shall glorify me: for he shall receive of mine, and shall shew it unto you." John 16:14

Commentary: The powers of healing, casting out evil spirits, and controlling the elements of nature and power over death. These powers testify of Jesus glory and divinity. The heavenly Father glorified his Son, and Jesus received it, as did the Holy Spirit. We through the Holy Spirit can also receive these spiritual gifts. It is very plain to see from these various scriptures that the Holy Spirit is the personal representative of Christ.

(6:7) God reveals the hidden secrets.

"But God hath revealed them unto us by his spirit: For the spirit searcheth all things, yea, the deep things of God." I Cor. 2:10

Commentary: Electricity was created by God, and it has always existed. One of nature's deep secretes. However, through divine intervention of God through the works of the Holy Spirit man was able to rediscover that which was hidden from us. Through deep study and research we were able to understand electricity and use it.

The Holy Spirit not only helps us to discover and understand some of the secrets of nature. But also helps us to discover the divine truth found in the Holy Scriptures. He helps us to understand the divine revelation of God's plans for man's salvation.

The Holy Spirit imparts understanding of truth to mankind. Once we submit ourselves to the guidance and illumination of the Holy Spirit. The Holy Spirit knows all things; he is a deity and member of the Godhead. He searches those who seek counsel and guidance, and brings them to the knowledge about God. It is the work of the Holy Spirit to share with man the things of God and bring his people into a state where they seek to investigate the truth.

(6:8) The Gospel was preached.

"…By them that have preached the gospel unto you with the Holy Spirit sent down from heaven; which things the angels desire to look into." I Peter 1:12

Commentary: The early Christian preachers of the New Testament gospel ministered unto their fellow man, and were closely associated with and by the spiritual influence of the Holy Spirit. They allowed themselves to be spiritually guided. St. Peter refers here to the mystical manifestation of *"Empathy,"* a mystical union between God and man. Both God and man exercise their freewill, free choice to join together, one thought, one mind.

(6:9) Between God and believers.

"Even the spirit of truth; whom the world cannot receive, because it seeth him not, neither knoweth him: but ye know him: for he dwelleth with you, and shall be in you." John 14:17

Commentary: Because the world can not see or touch the existence of the Holy Spirit, nor does the world know or understand the Holy Spirit. But you who truly believe know, for you feel him dwelling inside you. For it is written "For the Spirit of the Lord shall come upon you." Through this intimate union with the Holy Spirit, if you continue, shall bring about a change in your thinking, actions, words, feelings, the process of inner change, Sanctification. "The Spirit itself beareth witness with our Spirit, that we are the children of God." Romans 8:16

(6:10) Whose Presence will be with us when the Holy Spirit is upon us?

"I will not leave you comfortable: I will come to you." John 14:18

Commentary: What great promise did Jesus leave with his disciples? "Lo, I am with you always, even unto the end of the world." St. Matthew 28:20 Jesus will always be with us in spirit, and to those who study and practice what they are taught will truly know of his presence. Jesus knew in his bodily presence he could not be everywhere at once. But through the gift of the Holy Spirit it would be possible to be with his believer's throughtout the world, spiritually, even unto the end of time.

(6:11) Spiritual union among God, Jesus and man.

"At that day ye shall know that I am in my Father, and ye in me, and I in you." John 14:20

Commentary: Upon that day when you realize your need for Christ, then shall the Holy Spirit descent upon you, fill you, and you will know of the union between you and Christ. In that day the door to wisdom, knowledge, and spiritual understanding will be open to you. You will then obtain the fruits of the spirit and for those who seek it, the spiritual gifts of God.

(6:12) Warning to false teachers.

"*And the Lord said, my spirit shall not always strive with man.*" Genesis 6:3

Commentary: Those who teach the doctrine of men will lose the Holy Spirit. Those who seek to deceive the people of God for their own egotistic and selfish means will find emptiness within their very own beings because the Spirit of

God left them. Even King David's greatest fear was losing the Holy Spirit "Cast me not away from thy presence; and take not the Holy Spirit from me." Psalms 51:11

(6:13) Jesus spiritually enter believers.

"Behold, I stand at the door, and knock: if any man hear my voice, and open the door, I will come in to him, and will sup with him, and he with me." Revelation 3:20

Commentary: This is the door of salvation which man himself controls. For only he, through freedom of choice, can open this door and let him in.

Fruits of the Spirit

(6:14) The fruit of the Spirit?

"The fruit of the spirit is love, joy, peace, long-suffering, gentleness, goodness, faith, meekness, temperance." Galatians 5:22 & 23

Commentary: The fruit of the spirit is a manifestation of one's change, which naturally grows within us when we allow the Holy Spirit to influence and guide us. By nature we will become gentle creatures filled with love and joy for our fellow man. We will have faith and goodness and show temperance to evil doer and tempers. A whole new world will open up for us and we will see everything in a new light and find peace in our inner being.

(6:15) Works of the flesh?

"Now the works of the flesh are manifest, which are these; Adultery, fornication, uncleanness, lasciviousness, idolatry, witchcraft, hatred, variance, emulations, wrath, strife, seditions, heresies, envying, murders, drunkenness, reveling, and such like: of the which I tell you before, as I

have also told you in time past, that they which do such things shall not inherit the kingdom of God." Galatians 5:19 – 21

Commentary: The evil types of works that are listed above run parallel to the list found in St. Matthew 15:18-19, St. Mark 7:20-23, Romans 1:29-31, and II Timothy 3:1-5. These are the results of unrestricted operations of human emotions (passions, feelings, desires, etc.). There is nothing wrong with having, experience and enjoying these emotions. But when we allow them to become uncontrolled, only then do they become destructive, both physically and mentally, and can bring harm to yourself and others. In that respect it becomes evil.

(6:16) Avoiding the works of the flesh.

"Walk in the spirit, and ye shall not fulfill the lust of the flesh." Galatians 5:16

Commentary: Become spiritually minded with thoughts on God, and ideals of practicing spiritual truth and divine things. Walking with the Holy Spirit and feeling his influence and guidance, and following after him. By filling our lives with good deeds and practices and sharing them with others. By helping others and teaching them.

(6:17) Holy Spirit love.

"The love of God is shed abroad in our hearts by the Holy Spirit which is given to us." Romans 5:5

Commentary: This is the first time St. Paul mentions in his Epistle of the Holy Spirit. The presence and activity of the Holy Spirit in Christian growth and experiences is self evident, and the outpouring of the love in the hearts of Christians is a testifying of Jesus which He is the express image and likeness of the Father. The trinity of the three is one. If the Father is characterized as a God of love, then all three possess this same character.

(6:18) The Heavenly kingdom consist.

"For the kingdom of God is not meat and drink; but righteousness, and peace, and joy in the Holy Spirit." Romans 14:17

Commentary: A special joy and gladness is experienced by those who live in the spirit. "If we live in the Spirit, let us also walk in the Spirit." Galatians 5:25 Those Christians whose faith is the strongest, understand the heavenly kingdom best. What are most important are the spiritual grace, and not the material things of this world. Many people and even some so called Christians would rather regard their freedom of eating, drinking and enjoying the physical pleasure of the world more than being involved in the spiritual blessing and live their lives in the light of the Holy Spirit.

(6:19) Christians who practice a meek and quiet spirit.

"Whose adorning... let it be the hidden man of the heart... and the ornament of a meek and quiet spirit, which is in the sight of God of great price." I Peter 3:3 & 4

Commentary: The inward person, the true self of one's character and personality of the Christian faith who practice the art of humility, becomes meek and having a quiet and gentle spirit. They do not concern themselves with outward appearance, but understand that God looks inward upon the heart. These are the true Christians of the heavenly kingdom.

(6:20) The virtues of the fruit of the Holy Spirit.

"Against such there is no law." Galatians 5:23

Commentary: One who lives and practices the fruit of the spirit, against such there is no law to condemn them, for they are living within the guideline of the law.

(6:21) Unity of the Spirit.

"Endeavoring to keep the unity of the spirit in the bond of peace." Ephesians 4:3

Commentary: Between the trinity of the Godhead and the existence of man exists a unity of spirit. Those who understand this existence earnestly are always striving to maintain and strengthen this unity as well as learn how to use it. Peace to obtained when we practice the fruits of the spirit.

Gifts of the Holy Spirit

(6:22) As Christians, be concerned.

"Now concerning spiritual gifts brethren, I would not have you ignorant." I Cor. 12:1

Commentary: St. Paul was here concerned about the various gifts many of the early Christians received, how they were abusing them, the misunderstanding and rivalry between them (I Cor. 12:1-14).

The Spirit of God has always been within man, since the beginning of creation. So the gifts of the Holy Spirit existed in both Old and New Testament times. All spiritual gifts come from God for the purpose of manifesting the power of God, and to carry out His divine plan or purpose. All of this is so done to better and benefit the human race. We as creatures of God, blessed by being created after the likeness and image of our Creator, are his instruments for divine intervention. These gifts of manifestation are given to every man to profit withal "But the manifestation of the Spirit is given to every man to profit withal." I Cor. 12:7

(6:23) Christ enters heaven and man receives.

"Wherefore he saith, when he ascended up on high, he led captivity captive and gave gifts unto men." Ephesians 4:8

Commentary: Upon Christ's ascension, he took with him many captives and gave them gifts. Here it is referred to those people who were held captive in death. But he also gave spiritual gifts to those apostles who remain to form the Christian Church.

(6:24) Christ gave gifts.

"And he gave some the gifts to become apostles; and some prophets; and some evangelist; and some pastors and teachers." Ephesians 4:11

Commentary: *The Greek word "He" is emphatic, meaning "He himself" personally gave these gifts through the method of empathy, a* unity of feeling (see the first order of divinity "the holy scriptures part II question 2). Each position or title listed above has a purpose and performs a duty for the Church and its congregation, and for man as a whole.

(6:25) The result of these gifts.

"Till we all come into the unity of the faith, and the knowledge of the Son of God, unto a perfect man, unto the measure of the stature of the fullness of Christ." Ephesians 4:13

Commentary: These gifts will persist until the second coming of Christ, for the perfection of the faith, binding together all who believe these writings of mine and practice them. The word "perfection" in verse 12 suggests an ordered ministry of the Church. The word unity here is applied to both our faith in Christ, and our knowledge of him as God. In verse 12 it mentions the "Work of the ministry" this means all types of ministry and services within this faith, whether it's doctrine, teaching, prophecy, healing, and Church services of the Holy Sacraments.

(6:26) The manifestation of the one spirit.

"But the manifestation of the spirit is given to every man to profit withal, for to one is given by the spirit to word of wisdom; to another the word of knowledge by the same spirit; to another faith by the same spirit; to another the gift of healing by the same spirit; to another the working of miracles; to another prophecy; to another discerning of spirits; to another divers kinds of tongues; to another the interpretation of tongues. But all these worketh that one and the selfsame spirit, dividing to every man severally as his will." I Cor. 12:7-11

Commentary: The manifestation of the one spirit is understood to reveal the Holy Spirit in his true nature and operations. As he imparts these gifts, they are given to every man whom he feels will fulfill the measure that is needed to accomplish the divine goal. Let's review each of the spiritual gifts that St. Paul writes about.

1. **Word of Wisdom**: The gift of understanding the Holy Scriptures and the working of God. The man who possess this gift not only understands the Scriptures, but arranges his teaching in a way which he is able to explain his revelation to others.

2. **Word of Knowledge:** The gift of knowledge or the understanding of truth is knowing the facts. Again, understanding spiritual truth, then arranging it in a new orderly manner to better express one's thoughts to others. Spiritual knowledge is obtained by two ways. 1. Studying the Holy Scriptures and total giving your whole self to

God, and 2. Direct communication through divine inspiration.

3. **Faith:** This is not generally accepted faith that all Christian experience and confess. It is that special kind of faith that one experiences with a very deep passion of faith which enables its possessor to go forth and do exceptional things, works, for the Lord *"...and though I have all faith, so that I could remove mountains, and have not love, I am nothing."* I Cor. 13:2. All priests, pastors, ministers, and rabbis of the Lord must have love in their heart along with faith, to be effective in doing God's work. (See St. Matthews 17:20-21).

4. **Gift of healing**: This gift gives the possessor special powers such as indicated and exercised by the apostles "...they shall lay hands on the sick, and they shall recover." St. Mark 16:18 (See Acts 3:2-8 and 4:8-10). It is the right and privilege of all men to pray and ask for spiritual healing. But the gift of healing must be distinguished here. For a person has been chosen by God to be his instrument. The possessor receives divine knowledge and direction in his work. Other healer work for themselves, teaching that their power comes from within themselves and not from God.

5. **Gift of prophecy:** The divine psychic ability to foresee future events of people, historical events, and events of nations. The person who possesses this gift speaks with the authority for God, or in God's behalf, declaring God's will (See exodus 3:10, 14, 15; Deut. 18:15, 18; II Samuel 23:2; St. Matthew 11:9 & 10; and II Peter 1:21). Prophecy is a method chosen by God to establish a form of communication between God and man. (See numbers 12:6 and Amos 3:7). The entire Holy Bible came to man in just this same manner, through prophecy of revelation (See II Timothy 3:16 and II Peter 1:20, 21). The spirit of

prophecy is called the testimony of Jesus (See Rev. 12:17 and St. John 5:39). By means of visions, dreams, inspiration (empathy), and divine illumination of mind (contemplation) are some of the ways in which the gift of prophecy is given. Thus the prophet of God becomes his personally chosen spokesmen (See II Samuel 23:2; St. Matthew 3:3 and II Peter 1:21).

6. **Discerning of spirits**: This gift helps the possessor to distinguish between divine inspiration and counterfeit, temptation of the devil. Christ foretells in the last days, the rise of false prophets. He warns us of these prophets and their false teachings (See St. Matthew 24:4 & 5).

7. **Kinds of Tongues**: Many believe this to be taken as one having the ability to speak the language of angels. It is not so. Other believes it to speak a special language chosen by God, not so. It means that when you are in a room full of people, each person being born in a different language can understand you when you speak. For each person understands you in there own language in which they were born. In several churches I have witness a person worked up and starts speaking in gibberish tongues, and know one can understand them. This type of false speaking in tongues serves no purpose, and it is not what God had intended when He imparted the gift of speaking in tongues. The miracle here is the able to speak and everyone understands you in there own language. On Pentecost the Holy Spirit descended upon the apostles and they started to speak with other tongues, meaning other languages. (Reed Acts 2: 1-12). God does not dispense nonsense; he communicates in a clear and understanding manor that all his creatures can understand his will.

Note: Some people go to a revival meeting and sees a person standing and speaking in tongues, and because they can feel the power, the energy, that it is real it has to come from God, not so. They may witness spiritual healing of faith, and I know that God is working here, not always so. Satan has powers also, and at times he inmates God to a fine point that the average person can not discern between what comes from God and what is false and emanates from Satan. "For there shall arise false Christ, and false prophets, and shall shew great signs and wonder; insomuch that, if it were possible, they shall deceive the very elect." St. Matthew 24:24 The scriptures does not give us much information on the subject of speaking in tongues to properly define it, understand its purpose, nor how to test it to see if it comes from God.

The danger here is that many people get excited and rapped up emotionally in what they see and witness, instead of viewing it intelligently with their mind and through what they studied from the scriptures. Because emotions can lead to misconception, and lead to believing in false doctrines, so God gave us a mind to think and his Holy Scriptures as a reference, test the things we witness and see. We are to walk and believe in faith, yet guard ourselves against false doctrines "These were more noble than those in Thessalonica, in that they received the word with all readiness of mind, and search the scriptures daily, whether those things were so." Acts 17:11 Also we read in the Holy Scriptures "Study to shew thyself approved unto God, a workman that needeth not to be ashamed, rightly dividing the word of truth." II Timothy 2:15

People who study the Holy Bible are not taken easily and think with their head before establishing their faith.

8. **Interpretation of Tongues**: One who has the gift of understanding and interpreting various languages.

Outpouring of the Holy Spirit

(6:27) Christ promise his disciples.

"And behold, I send the promise of my Father upon you: but tarry ye in the city of Jerusalem, until ye be endued with power from on high." Luke 24:49

Commentary: The promise of the Father is the Holy Spirit (Acts 1:4,8). Jesus says "With Power" the ability to perform, as effective witnesses (See verse 48). The early disciple had to receive some kind of heavenly power; to help them convince the people what they witnessed was the truth. That the event witnessed did really happen. They themselves had to receive courage and confidence within, in order to go forth and witness for Jesus. With the works of the Holy Spirit the church experienced fast growth and conversion.

(6:28) Baptism was foretold.

"Ye shall be baptized with the Holy Spirit not many days hence." Acts 1:5

Commentary: This self-same promise was given by St. John the Baptist as foretold. "I indeed baptize you with water unto repentance: But he that cometh after me is mightier that I, whose shoes I am not worthy to bear: he shall baptize you with the Holy Spirit, and with fire." Matthew 3:11. Baptism is a symbolic act, but it also has power. Baptism is an initiation into the Christian faith. It has the power to wash away the stain of original sin that was committed by our first parents "Adam & Eve". For adults who are being baptized for the first time, baptism will also wash away all sins they committed from birth up to the time of baptism. However, this type of baptism of which St. Luke writes about is greater than that done by water. It's the power of regeneration of our soul, where it overcomes the person, filling him as an eternal well, which exists in all of us.

(6:29) Holy baptism and God ministry.

"But ye shall receive power, after the Holy Spirit is come upon you: and ye shall be witness unto me both in Jerusalem, and in all Judea, and in Samaria, and unto the uttermost part of the earth." Acts 1:8

Commentary: Once the Holy Spirit has descended upon the disciples they shall receive power. It also provided the disciple courage, confidence, and leadership. The power of witnessing gives us three benefits: 1. Internal power of faith, courage, self-confidence; 2. The skill to teach and witness the gospel; and 3. The gift of influence, to lead others to God.

Through spiritual union between Jesus and his disciple (empathy) Christ was still able to continue his work of salvation. What does it mean, to witness? From the Greek "Martures" those who have seen, heard, or know, for themselves the truth they share.

(6:30) The day of Pentecost.

"Now when they heard this, they pricked in their heart, and said,… men and brethren, what shall we do? Then Peter said unto them, repent, and be baptized every one of you in the name of Jesus Christ for the remission of sins, and ye shall receive the gift of the Holy Spirit… then they that gladly received his word were baptized: and the same day there were added unto them about three thousand souls." Acts 2:37-41

Commentary: At Pentecost the disciples believed and by their faith were baptized and were ordained by God for the effective preaching of his words for the conviction and faith to man (See Romans 10:17 and I Cor. 1:21). When the disciples were "pricked" they were painfully (mentally) sorrowful about their sins and resulted in true repentance

(See I Cor. 7:9-11). They went forth and preached the Gospel and many people repented and were converted to Christianity.

At Pentecost the Holy Spirit came upon the twelve apostles, and received special spiritual gifts, and the authority of holy church. In the teachings of the Roman and Orthodox Catholic Church, the authority and spiritual gifts were handed down from apostles to bishops and from bishops to priests, by the laying on of hands. Only through apostolic succession, the unbroken line of bishops from which the power of the Holy Spirit acts through, Bishops being able to trace their lineage back to one of the twelve apostles, making all holy sacraments valid. It is very important that the link of apostolic succession be unbroken, so the transfer of spiritual gifts and authority can be properly handed down. Once the person is consecrated "by the laying on of hands" and the apostolic succession is passed onto the person, it can never be undone. Ordination is forever.

Now some Protestant Churches also have apostolic succession such as the Church of England, The Old Catholic Church, Episcopal Church, Lutheran Church, United Methodist, and other independent Churches.

As for the Protestant churches as a whole, believer they get their authority from the Holy Scriptures themselves, and follow the teaching of Christ, according to what is written the Bible. Yet, I found many Churches practicing and believing what they want to believe and not always what God says we should believe or do.

The Seventh Order of Divinity

"The Holy Trinity"

I John Paul, a Servant of Christ Jesus, by the grace of God, write this Bible commentary on the *Holy Trinity*. My blessings go with you, peace from God our Father and from our Lord and Saviour Jesus of Nazareth called the Christ. The trinity is a joining or divine union of three deities, forming the Godhead, or God-hood. The word "tri" comes to us from the Latin or Greek meaning three, having, combining, or involving three. In the Christian theology and in the teaching of the Christian Talmud, the Godhead consist of three divine beings (Creators), the Father, the Son, and the Holy Spirit, all having a divine nature, possessing powers of divinity, all made of the same spiritual essence and being of the same substance.

This doctrine of the Holy Trinity is one of the great fundamentals of all Christianity. Three deities together in one spiritual union, having one mind, working toward one goal, one ideal, one purpose, having one understanding. Yet, each having or maintaining his own identity, personality, and character. Each holding his own place having his own purpose and function in the divine government of the Godhead.

In the teaching of Judaism, a monotheism religion of the Jewish faith is the belief in one God "Hear, O Israel: The Lord our God is one Lord." Deut. 6:4 The Christian faith is an off shoot of the Jewish faith, but received greater enlightenment, because it expanded and fulfilled the theology and prophecy of the Old Testament, thereby expounding the theology of the Godhead. Through the teaching of Jesus Christ, the Christian Church is able to advance beyond the Jewish theology about God. The Holy Trinity is the central focus of Jesus teaching, a theology of their being only one God, but three distinct divine persons in that existence. Each being equal in majesty, undivided in splendor, one Lord, one God.

The Holy Trinity

(7:1) Christ posses power and authority of divinity.

"For in him dwelleth all the fullness of the Godhead bodily." Colossians 2:9

Commentary: St. Paul makes it clear here that in Jesus, dwells the sum total of the divine nature and all attributes of God. Possessing all powers of deity such as creativity, and all the qualities such as dignity, authority, Excellency, and love. In all fullness the power and quality of God is not limited to time, space, and power.

(7:2 The Godhead.

"Go ye therefore, and teach all nations, baptizing them in the name of the Father, and of the Son, and of the Holy Spirit." Matthew 28:19

Commentary: We are commanded to go out and make disciples of both the Jews and the Gentiles, of all nations, and bring them into the family of God. Jesus here states three deities, The Father, The Son, and The Holy Spirit, naming three distinct persons. The Holy Trinity is a complete mystery to us and we can only give opinion as to the deep of their existence.

(7:3) Union between members and God.

"I go unto the Father: for my Father is greater than I" I John 14:28

Commentary: Jesus power and authority was equal unto the Father "Who, being in the form of God, thought it not robbery to be equal with God." Philippians 2:16 (See St. John 1:1-3) in his pre-incarnation state. But in humility he himself declared the greatness of the Father, for Jesus "But made himself of no reputation, and took upon him the form of a servant." Philippians 2:7 (See Hebrew 2:9).

Each one having a purpose working for one goal, one plan of action. However, Jesus in his incarnation declared that he was with the Father "I and my Father are one." John 10:30 After his crucifixion the Father exalted his Son and gave him a name above every name "Wherefore God also hath highly exalted him, and given him a name which is above every name" Philippians 2:9. He was then equal with the Father (See I Cor. 15:27, 28 and 11:3).

Characteristic of a Deity

(7:4) The characteristic of the sons of God.

1. Omnipotent: *"For the Lord God omnipotent reigneth"* Rev. 19:6

Commentary: Omnipotent meaning the "Almighty", "All powerful", taken from the Greek "Pantokrator" means "A ruler of all" this title recurs many time in revelations 4:8; 11:17; 15:3; 16:7; 19:6 translated at times as "Omnipotent."

2. Omnipresent: *"For the eyes of the Lord run to and fro throughout the whole earth"* II Chronicles 16:9 (See Zechariah 4:10).

Commentary: God sees everywhere. He sees everything, through his spirit, his presence can be felt anywhere. As Biblical scholars state "all seeing" We are created beings, and the Spirit of God lives within us, and through our inner union with him he knows our thoughts, he experiences our sorrow, he is apart of our inner most feelings.

3. Omniscient: *"…The only wise God…"* I Timothy 1:17

Commentary: Through the union of spirit between God and man, wisdom can be obtained. Everything in the universe has already been created. However, through our spiritual union with the Creator, man rediscovers what God had already created, and obtains understanding through readiness of mind.

4. Immutable: "Wherein God, willing more abundantly to shew unto the heirs of promise the immutability of his counsel, confirmed it by an oath." Hebrews 6:17

Commentary: One of God's divine nature is that He is unchanging. In counsel he confirmed to mediate, taken from the Greek "Mesiteno," means, "to guarantee." An oath or given word of promises.

Once a covenant has been made, he confirms it, then it becomes unchanging on his part, because this is part of his nature.

5. Eternal: *"His dominion is an everlasting dominion."* Daniel 7:14

Commentary: God's existence cannot be measured in time or space. He is eternal. He has no beginning and no end. *"I Am that I Am,"* He is God.

The three divine being of the Holy Trinity is one in substance (essence), in love, and in divine purpose. Jesus voluntarily submitted himself to the will of the Father, in order that he might become incarnated in human flesh. Taking upon himself man's nature, and becoming the second

Adam. Through this act of love he has atoned for man's original sin when he was crucified. He now intercedes for us in heaven as our representative before God. Even though our finite minds cannot understand the infinite and divine, we still live secure in the knowledge that Christ, our Saviour will be eternal (See I Cor. 15:24-28). And salvation is a real promise.

The Lord our God is one God (Deut. 6:4), in the personage of three beings, all of the same substance. The Holy Trinity having three persons: The Father is the source of the Godhead, He is the principle of the unity between the three. He is born of none and proceeds from none. The Son (Jesus) is the only begotten Son, born of the Father from the beginning, from all eternity, before all ages. Jesus is the incarnated God, who shows his loving kindness toward man. Maybe we can look at the trinity from a human viewpoint. It has long been known that humans can have a split personally. One moment he can be one person, and the next few minutes he can be another person, totally unaware of the other personality. We can view God as being one person, possessing three distinct personages in a total divine manner, beyond our complete understanding. Christ himself said that God is a Spirit and must be worship in Spirit (St. John 4:24), so the divine substance or divine essence, is Spirit.

Jesus, as the divine Son of God, through his great at of love, came down from heaven and was incarnated into flesh, He now possess two types of nature. 1. A divine nature, and 2. A human nature. This theology is very interesting. In the Christian faith when the world was created our first parents (Adam & Eve), failed the test of obedience and was cast our of Eden. The Creator loved his creation so much that He was willing to sacrifice apart of himself (the Son), so that we his creature can have eternal life with him. The Christian faith is the only religion that I know of that the deity came down to earth took the place of Adam and died for us all, a divine act. It was a divine law that condemns us and it had to be the death of a divine being to pay the price of the stain of Original Sin.

The nature of Jesus Christ, being one person living with two natures, without any kind of separation, merged together without any kind of confusion. One person endowed with two "wills."

The Holy Spirit is the third person of the trinity. He proceeds from the Father "But when the Comforter is come, whom I will send unto you from the Father, even the Spirit of truth, which proceedeth from the Father, he shall testify of me." John 15:26 from all eternity, sent by the Son as a Comforter.

6. Love: *"For God is love."* I John 4:8

Commentary: Love is an essential quality or attribute of God's nature. Because a man who loves not is fellow man, does not know God. This is a sign of proof or a test of one's knowledge of God. His love is great and unchanging.

7. Merciful: *"The Lord, the Lord God, merciful and gracious."* Exodus 34:6

Commentary: The Lord God, full of mercy and grace, great emphasis must be placed upon mercy because our relationship to him is based upon mercy. It is through this unchanging character of God that give the poor, helpless, and the needy great hope of eternal life (Psalms 103:8-14; 145:8; and Jeremiah 29:11; 31:3).

8. Just: *"Just and right is he."* Deut. 32:4

Commentary: In all truth, his Judgements are just. He is fair and just in all his works and counsel (Rev. 15:3).

The Eight Order of Divinity

"The Angelic Host"

I John Paul, a Servant of Christ Jesus, by the Grace of God, write this commentary on the *Angelic Host.* My blessings are upon you and peace from God our Father and from our Lord Jesus of Nazareth called the Christ. The word angel comes from the Hebrew "Mal' ak" and from the Greek "Aggelos" which means messenger. Angels are supernatural beings created by God possessing great spiritual powers far beyond that of man's ability.

Ministry of Good Angels

(8:1) St. Paul commits on the heavenly family.

"For this cause I bow my knees unto the Father of our Lord Jesus Christ, of whom the whole family in heaven and earth is named." Ephesians 3: 14 & 15

Commentary: There has been scholarly discussion of the phrase "whole family," because from the Greek this phrase can be translated as whole family or as every family. It is spiritual understanding that the proper translation is "Every Family" for every family in heaven and on earth, shall become one family of God and bear the name of the Heavenly Father name.

(8:2) Members of the heavenly family

"Behold, what manner of love the Father hath bestowed upon us, that we should be called the sons of God." I John 3:1

Commentary: Through the process of spiritual rebirth (St. John 3:1-12), we (man) can become the divine children of

God, members of his earthly family. Everyone, who comes to Christ and learns of him, believes in him, and in faith and love follows his footsteps can become a member of his heavenly family, the sons of God. I am lost in the wonder of it all, and as I contemplate the measureless height and depth of God's divine love.

When I practiced as a priest of the Old Catholic Church some of my parishioners would tell me that they would see a white light surround me, emitting from by body when I celebrated the Lord Supper (Mass). Not everyone sees this white light, only those tuned in at the time. At the climax of the Lords support when the Holy Spirit descends upon the elements, I am in a state of grace. I am so captivated by the magnitude of divine affection that it fills my heart, as it should fill the hearts of all bishops, priests, ministers, and of all Christian people.

(8:3) The heavenly family is called.

"And I beheld, and I heard the voice of many angels." Revelation 5:11

Commentary: In the first epistle of St. John 3:1 we learn that men who become spiritual sons of God are God's earthly family who one day will join the ranks and become one with the heavenly family. The heavenly family is the angels of God.

(8:4) angels before man fall.

"So he drove out the man: and he placed at the east of the Garden of Eden Cherubim's (angel), and a flaming sword, which turned every way, to keep the way of the tree of life." Genesis 3:24

Commentary: According to the Bible, Cherubim's belong to a class of supernatural being known as angels. Angels did exist before man was cast out of the Garden of Eden. For when sin entered the world, because of man disobedience to God, angels were sent to guard the tree of life so sinful man would not gain immortality.

(8:5) Numbering the Heavenly Host.

"But ye are come unto Mount Sinai and unto the city of the living God, the heavenly Jerusalem, and to an innumerable company of angels." Hebrews 12:22

"A fiery stream issued and came forth from before him: thousand thousands ministered unto him, and ten thousand times ten thousand stood before him: the judgement was set, and the books were opened." Daniel 7:10

Commentary: In the days of Daniel and St. Paul, ten thousand times ten thousand was a very large number, and was meant to express a large number of angels, a number unable to have a count. Even at the Second Coming of Christ, Jesus will come with a large number of angels (St. Mathew 25:31).

(8:6) Angelic Host higher than Man.

"For thou hast made him a little lower than the angels." Psalms 8:5

Commentary: Before man fell from the state of grace, he was a created being, created higher than the holy angels were. I say this because we were created in the likeness and image of God (Genesis 1:26). The angels were not created after the likeness and image of God. After man was cast out of the Garden of Eden, man lost that special image or likeness that God to this day retains. The state of grace, which I am talking about here, is the spiritual or divine mirror or condition or state of man's soul living in or having habitual grace. According to the translation of this verse from the following manuscripts of the Greek versions "Aquila" and the "Symmachus" and the "Theodation and from the Latin "Vulgate" all translate this verse using the word God rather than angels.

Also according to the Hebrew and Chaldee dictionary found in the Strong's exhaustive concordance the word that is written by the writer of this verse in psalms is "Elohim" which is translated as God. The word "Me' Elohim" comes from the Hebrew which literally means "Than God." However, after man fell from the state of grace, he was cast out of the garden even though his consciousness was elevated to the point of understanding, his soul became stained and man fell below the level of the angels. Even man's physical began to age and change. "Thou madest him a little lower than the angels; thou crownedst him with glory and honour, and didst set him over the works of thy hands." Hebrew 2:7 This verse is not talking about man, but about Christ. If we would read verse six *"…or the son of man, that thou visitest him?"* it talks about the son of man, and there is only one son of man and that is Jesus Christ. So Paul writes in his book to the Hebrews that Christ was made lower than the angels, not created, but made, for a little while.

We find in verse nine that Paul's writing becomes clear "But we see Jesus, who was made a little lower than the angels for the suffering of death, crowned with glory and honour…" Hebrew 2:9 During Christ incarnation He was made lower than the angels.

(8:7) Angels are subject to God.

"Who is gone into heaven, and is on the right hand of God; angels and authorities and powers being made subject unto him." I Peter 3:22

Commentary: Upon ascension Jesus entered into his glory with his Father, and now sits at the right hand of God. All things and powers in this universe are placed at his feet and is now subject unto his authorities, for he has paid the price and fulfilled the prophecy. Angels and man are subject unto Christ, but this is done of free choice of the angels and of man. We are speaking of a higher spiritual order of understanding and love.

(8:8) Entertain strangers.

"Be not forgetful to entertain strangers: for thereby some have entertained angels unaware." Hebrews 13:2

Commentary: Angels have the power to take on human form, this is one way they are able to help us, deliver messages, or depart words of inspiration from God. Angels are beautiful creatures of God, and each one of us has an angel, who watches over us, a guardian angel.

The Character, Power, and Works of Angels

(8:9) Angelic strength and character.

"Bless the Lord, ye his angels, that excel in strength, that does his commandments, hearkening unto the voice of his word." Psalms 103:20

Commentary: The angels of God, themselves keep his commandments, they excel in strength and in character because of it. Both the angels in heaven (heavenly family) and the human race (earthly family) obey the Lord's commandments, binding them together as one big family of God, making us the obedient ones of God, the commandment-keeping children.

(8:10) The work of angels.

"Are they not all ministering spirits sent forth to minister for them who shall be heirs of salvation." Hebrew 1:14

Commentary: From the Greek *"Leitourgikos"* means "rendering service" this word is also related to *"Leitourgos"* which is translated ministers. So the proper translation is that angels of God render public service to mankind. Man is the heir of salvation, and the angels of heaven will minister unto us.

(8:11) Jacob dream

"And he dreamed, and behold a ladder set upon the earth, and the top of it reached to heaven: and behold the angels of God ascending and descending on it." Genesis 28:12

Commentary: This dream has a symbolic meaning. The ladder, which touches the earth and reaches unto heaven, is a visible symbol of real and the uninterrupted fellowship between God in heaven and his people on earth. The angels who ascend into heaven are taking our petitions before God and the angels, which descend with the promises of divine help and protection.

(8:12) Our guardian angel

"Take heed that ye despise not one of these little ones; for I say unto you, that in heaven their angels do always behold the face of my Father which is in heaven." Matthew 18:10

Bible reference: Psalms 103:20, 21 and Hebrew 1:14

Commentary: Each of us has an angel assigned to us by God to watch over us, and protect us from evil. The Old Hebrew idiomatic usage of words *"behold the face"* means to have access to him. Angels of God always have access to him. Angels of God always have access to the presence of God, to deliver our petitions before God for divine assistance "The righteous cry, and the Lord heareth, and delivereth them out of all their troubles." Psalms 34:17

(8:13) Biblical symbol of a Chariots?

"The chariots of God are twenty thousand, even thousand of Angels." Psalms 68:17

Commentary: This is a useful understanding when studying Bible prophecy. A chariot is a symbolic sign, which is interpreted to mean angels.
The word angels in psalms 68:17 is taken from the Hebrew word *"Shin'an"* which is rendered in the Authorized Version as angels. However, in other translations it is render as "Change" or "Repetition." The word may be closely related to ugaritic, a Semitic language closely related to classical Hebrew *"Shin'tinn"* meaning "Warrior." The warriors of God are then the Angelic Host.

(8:14) Angels protect us.

"The angel of the Lord encampeth round about them that fear him, and delivereth them." Psalms 34:7

Commentary: The continual presence of our guardian angel is one of our sweetest assurances. It is our right as God's children of the Old and New Testament, for it is our heritage as true Christians.

(8:15) Apostles delivered from prison

"But the angel of the Lord by night opened the prison doors, and brought them forth." Acts 5:19

Commentary: St. Luke here records a supernatural intervention, as an angel of God appeared and opened up the door and freed the apostles, angels do exist and do help us. We must remain strong in our faith.

(8:16) Elijah strengthened by ministry of angels

"And the angel of the Lord came again the second time, and touched him, and said, arise and eat…" I King 19:7

Commentary: The journey, which the prophet Elijah had to make, was great and difficult, and the angel of the Lord provided food and drink for him to help him in his journey.

(8:17) Angels minister to Christ.

"Then the devil leaveth him, and behold, angels came and ministered unto him" St. Matthew 4:11 and in the Garden of Gethsemane "And there appeared an angel unto him from heaven, strengthening him." Luke 22:43

Commentary: After the temptation of Satan, while hunger weighted heavy upon him, Jesus was exhausted as he fell to the earth. Then angels ministered *unto* him. Because of his obedience to his Father, and the assurances of his Father" love along with the joy of all heaven in his victory over Satan" temptation, gave him great comfort and it strengthened him. We too as true Christians have the assurance of our guardian angel to minister and strengthen us in times of great temptations.

In the knowledge of understanding, we too can find comfort in our victory over Satan's temptation. As a result, this will motivate us to continue on our path to a holy life.

(8:18) Angelic Joy.

"I say unto you, there is joy in the presence of the angels of God over one sinner that repenteth." Luke 15:10

Commentary: Joy from our Father in heaven as well as from our guardian angel is expressed when we repent our sins and give them up. When on repents, it means he has experienced a change in his heart. He understands the evil of his doing (sin) and feels sorrow for his actions. This is true repentance. Once true repentance is experienced, he forsakes (give up) his sinful life. Then all of heaven rejoices in his repentance and our heavenly Father welcomes us with open arms.

(8:19) God's protection.

"There shall be no evil befall thee, neither shall any plague come nigh thy dwelling. For he shall give angels charge over thee, to keep in all thy ways." Psalms 91:10 & 11

Commentary: The promise of the Lord is in truth and it is real, for his angels have charge over us to protect us from evil. This protection is only as strong as our faith.

Angelic Host

(8:20) Angels surround the throne of God.

"And I beheld, and I heard the voice of many angels round about the throne." Rev. 5:11

Commentary: The obedient angels of heaven exist in a total state of grace, and are able to stand in the presence of God's glory, without being consumed. The obedient angels of God exists without the stain of sin, they are pure in heart, mind, and spirit.

(8:21) Angels as created beings

"For by him were all things created, that are in heaven, and that are in earth, visible and invisible…" Colossians 1:16

Commentary: All things in our universe, including those in heaven are created, all visible and invisible things and creatures. This verse includes the angels, as created beings, pure and supernatural.

(8:22) Angels are beings of dazzling brilliance.

"For the angels of the Lord descended from heaven, and came and rolled back the stone from the door, and sat upon it. His countenance was like lightning, and his raiment white as snow." Matthew 28:2 & 3

Commentary: Angels are supernatural creatures that are pure illumines beings, surrounded by a brilliant white light. Many times this radiant light was taken as fire by the Old Testament prophecy. This white light, by some scholars is taken to be the glory of God, a state of existence without sin.

(8:23) Angels are beings of great beauty.

"Thine heart was lifted up because of thy beauty, thou hast corrupted thy wisdom by reason of thy brightness." Ezekiel 28:17

Commentary: In this verse God is talking to Satan and telling him he was created beautiful and because of his brilliant state of existence, he allowed himself to become intoxicated by his own beauty, thus wanting to become equal unto God.

(8:24) Angels can travel at great speed.

"And the living creatures ran and returned as the appearance of a flash of lightning." Ezekiel 1:14

Commentary: According to the above verse it seems that angels can travel as fast as lightning, which is the same as saying they are able to travel at the speed of light. According to our understanding of today's physics, light travels at 186, 000,00 miles per second.

(8:25) Angels have great powers.

"And it came to pas that night, that the angel of the Lord went out, and smote in the camp of the Assyrians an hundred fourscore and five thousand: and when they arose early in the morning, behold, they were all dead corpses." II King 19:35

Commentary: It took only one angel of the Lord to smite five thousand and one hundred and eighty men, all in one night. Such a power that an angel can hold within his hands.

(8:26) Angels are able to take on other life forms.

"Be not forgetful to entertain strangers: thereby some have entertained angels unaware." Hebrews 13:2

Commentary: Angels are able to take on human form, at times to carry on their ministry, and to fulfill their mission.

(8:27) Angels have wings.

"And when they went, I heard the noise of their wings, like the noise of great water, as the voice of the Almighty, the voice of speech, as the noise of an host: when they stood, they let down their wings." Ezekiel 1:24

Commentary: Angels do have wings. Some angels have two wings; others have four wings, even six wings. "Above it stood the Seraphim: each one had six wings; with two he covered his face, and with two he covered his feet, and with two he did fly." Isaiah 6:2 The Seraphim are the highest form of angels in the realm or Orders of angels. No where does the Bible describe what kind of wings do angels have. Are the wings of the angels, like that of a bird with feathers, or are their wings fashioned after that of a butterfly type wings?

(8:28) Angels are invisible spirits.

"And the ass saw the angel of the Lord standing in the way, and his sword drawn in his hand: and the ass turned aside out of the way, and went into the field: and Balaam smote the ass, to turn her into the way…Then the Lord opened the eyes of Balaam, and he saw the angel of the Lord standing in the way, and his sword drawn in his hand." Numbers 22:22-31

Commentary: Balaam was riding is donkey along the road when his donkey saw an angel of the Lord with his sword drawn, and the donkey went into the nearby field. Now Balaam did not see the angel of the Lord, but the donkey did. After Balaam smote the ass, then the Lord open Balaam eyes and he was then able to see the angel.

(8:29) Jesus taught of Angels.

"The Son of man shall send forth his angels." Matthew 13:41 Also *"Take heed that ye despise not one of these little ones; for I say unto you, That in heaven their angels do always behold the face of my Father which is in heaven."* Matthew 18:10 Also *For in the resurrection they neither marry, nor are given in marriage, but are as the angels of God in heaven."* St. Matthew 22:30 Also *"Likewise, I say unto you, there is joy in the presence of the angels of God over one sinner that repenteth."* Luke 15:10

Commentary: The above scriptures show that Jesus believed in angels and taught about them. If Jesus, the Son of God taught about angels then angels are real.

Dark Ministry of Evil Angels

(8:30) Against whom do we wrestle with.

"For we wrestle not against powers, against the rulers of the darkness of this world, against spiritual wickedness in high places." Ephesians 6:12

Commentary: Our fight is not against blood and flesh (man) but against the evil forces and powers of Satan. For Satan made open rebellion against God and against (us) his children. St. Paul reminds us of this fact, that evil influences of Satan changes men into evil servants. (See Ephesians 6:13-18).

(8:31) Evil angels sent to Hell.

"For if God spared not the angels that sinned, but cast them down to hell, and delivered them into chains of darkness, to be reserved unto judgment." II Peter 2:4

Commentary: Many commentaries try to explain the existence of hell. The darkness in which the evil angels were cast can be in a dimension unknown by man, and entrance into this world can take place only under certain conditions. Only through special rituals and rites where a medium (man) invokes the powers of darkness, only then can a door open up to allow the evil one to enter this world (dimension). Rev. 12:9, 12 The Holy Scriptures state that these evil angels are chained to this darkness, meaning they can not leave this world (realm), without the help of another source or force to help them.

(8:32) Various Names of Satan.

"Hereafter I will not talk much with you: For the prince of this world cometh, and hath nothing in me." John 14:30

Commentary: Satan declares himself as the god of this world *And, the devil taketh him up into an exceeding high mountain, and sheweeth him all the Kingdom of the world, and the glory of him;*

and saith unto him, all these things will I give thee, if thou wilt fall down and worship me." Matthew 4:8,9 (See I John 5:19). However, God is the true sovereignty of this world. Satan will go under many different names, and we should recognize them if we are to become Biblical Scholars for the Lord. He will come under many forms, and through various mediums. Many ministers believe Satan has control over this world and its inhabitants. That people of the world for the most part follow the teachings, and yield themselves to his temptation and in some cases take part in his wickedness. People who willfully sin will be given over to Satan (See I Cor. 5:5 and I Timothy 1:20).

(8:33) Satan's main occupation.

"Be sober, be vigilant; because your adversary the devil, as a roaring lion, walketh about, seeking whom he may devour." I Peter 5:8

Commentary: Satan and his angels occupy their time in going about and seeking their prey. Evil angel some time, with help, may cross over unto our world, but then sent back when over come by the power of good. Even though they can't cross over physically, Satan still has power of influence. He literally seeks to change men's hearts so they may come to join his army, practice his evil ways, come to love evil instead of good, and turn from God. Satan is an angel that is pure evil, and drunk with power, and he exists in his own delusion of over throwing God, and taking over heaven. Only with the help of another source or force can a devil cross over the threshold and enter into our world.

(8:34) What should we not do?

"Be ye angry, and sin not; let not the sun go down upon your wrath: neither give place to the devil." Ephesians 4:26, 27

Commentary: The command here to be angry is of a righteous indignation, which stimulates men into warriors of God against evil. When Christians practice righteous indignation their anger is directed against the evil and wrong act, and not against the person who does wrong or evil. When you are able to separate the two, you as a Christian have achieved much in spiritual growth. Our second command is not to sin. A warning is issued to all Christian about righteous indignation becoming not so justifiable anger where one feels personal resentment. This is a safe guard against the abuse of righteous indignation, and never gives Satan a chance to tempt you into fear; confusion, revenge or resentment, for these things (emotions) destroys the soul (person).

(8:35) An increase in demoniacal manifestation?

"Woe to the inhabiters of the earth and of the seal for the devil is come down unto you, having great wrath, because he knoweth that he hath but a short time." Rev. 12:12

Commentary: Satan and his angels know what the Holy Scriptures says about them only having a short time. However, they being so engrossed in their delusion, that they don't believe the Holy Scriptures, and are going forth working signs of wonder to deceive the people of the earth.

(8:36) People will be misguided.

"Now the spirit speaketh expressly that in the latter times some shall depart from the faith, giving heed to seducing spirits, and doctrine of devils." I Timothy 4:1

Commentary: The Holy Spirit speaks to us through the Holy Scriptures and warns us of the latter days when seducing (or wandering) spirits (devils) will go about misleading and being deceptive and influence people to remove themselves from the Church and to apostatize themselves. Demons are great teachers of deception, they work to control the mind of men and teach them their evil doctrine.

(8:37) Satan, his devils and of wicked people reward.

"Depart from me, ye cursed, into everlasting fire, prepared for the devil and his angels." Matthew 25:41

Commentary: All of the wicked shall be with Satan and his angels, and shall share the same punishment, which is everlasting fire.

The Origin of Evil

(8:38) Sin originated.

"He that committeth sin is of the devil; for the devil sinneth from the beginning." I John 3:8

Commentary: The Scriptures is clear that Satan is the first being whom sin worked its evil Satan sinneth from the beginning.

(8:39) Satan and the act of murder.

"Ye are of your father the devil, and the lusts of your father ye will do. He was a murderer from the beginning." John 8:44

Commentary: The spirit of murder, being part of evil called sin, fell upon Lucifer, when he first rebelled against God and brought the sentence of death upon himself, and upon the angels that followed him, and finally upon the human race, thus making him the first murderer.

(8:40) Satan and the act of lying

"For he is a liar, and the father of it." John 8:44

Commentary: Satan's career as a liar began in heaven, where his falsehood and misrepresented the divine character of God before the entire heavenly host. His lies brought about the fall of our first parents "And the serpent said unto the woman, ye shall not surely die". Genesis 3:4

(8:41) Creation of Satan.

"Thou wast perfect in thy ways from the day that thou wast created, till iniquity was found in thee." Ezekial 28:15

Commentary: Satan was and still is a beautiful angel, a picture of a devil with horns is a false misconception of Satan. His nature was of divine origin until the nature of sin changed him and led him to banishment from heaven. He retains his powers and is limited to the earth only.

(8:42) Satan sinned.

1. Corruption

"Thine heart was lifted up because of thy beauty, thou hast corrupted thy wisdom by reason of thy brightness." Ezekial 28:17

2. Fall

"How art thou fallen from heaven, O Lucifer, son of the morning! How art thou cut down to the ground, which didst weaken the nation! For thou hast said in thine heart." Isaiah 14:12

3. Rebellion

"I will ascend into heaven, I will exalt my throne above the stars of God: I will sit also upon the mount of the congregation in the sides of the north; I will ascend above the heights of the clouds; I will be like the most high." Isaiah 14:13, 14

4. Cast to Hell

"Yet thou shalt be brought down to hell, to the sides of the pit." Isaiah 14:15

Commentary: Lucifer's pride and ego became more than he was able to handle, and he thought of himself greater than God. His desire for self-exaltation was the cause of his downfall. His desire to be part of the Godhead, to be divine, to be like God, equal. He desired the homage of all of God's creatures, yet he was a creature (a created being) himself. How can a creature think to be equal unto God?

Satanic Powers

(8:43) Power of Temptation.

"For we have not an high priest which cannot be touched with the feeling of our infirmities; but was in all points tempted like as we are, yet without sin." Hebrews 4:15 (see St. Matthew 4:3-11).

Commentary: Satan tempted Even Christ when he was here on earth, just as we are tempted now. Christ over came Satan temptation and through Christ we can also.

(8:44) Powers of Miracles.

"For there shall arise false Christ, and false prophets, and shall shew great signs and wonders…" Matthew 24:24

Commentary: In the latter days, just before the second coming of Christ, Satan will come upon the earth as a false Christ working great wonders and miracles.

(8:45) Powers to Possess.

"And Jesus rebuked the devil; and he departed out of him: and the child was cured from that very hour." Matthew 17:18 (See St. Mark 1:23-28 and St. Matthew 8:28-34).

Commentary: The child was possessed by one of Satan angel, also called devil, and Jesus cast him out and the child was cured.

(8:46) Power to take on animal form.

"Now the serpent was more subtle than any beast of the field which the Lord God had made. And he said unto the woman, yea, hath God said, ye shall not eat of every tree of the garden?" Genesis 3:1, 14, 15

Commentary: Of all the beast of the field, Satan has chosen to imitate the serpent, in order to temp Eve to disobey God command. A beautiful angel taking on the form of a serpent, to carry out his evil deeds. We must always be aware of Satan power of influence to trick us; we must guard ourselves against his evil powers.

(8:47) Power of transformation.

"And no marvel; for Satan himself is transformed into an angel of light." II Cor. 11:14

Commentary: In verse 13 we read that some men who are deceitful, will transform himself, change his outward appearance, to the point were he looks, talks, and acts like one of Christ apostles. So does Satan transform himself, to change his outward appearance, to make us think he is an angel of the Lord. We must always be on guard against Satan crafty skills, that he may appear as an angel of light, where in truth, he has no place in the divine realm of God's glory.

(8:48) Satan occupy his time

"Be sober, be vigilant; because your adversary the devil, as a roaring lion, walketh about, seeking whom he may devour." I Peter 5:8 (See Job 1:7)

Commentary: Satan, drunk in his own delusion, his mental forces moves about the seeking who he can trap into becoming one of his followers. Remember, he is bound in another dimension and can not appear to us in physical form, only through his mental powers can he tempt us, or through the use of his spiritual powers can he possess humans, but only those who allow it.

(8:49) Satan's methods of evil.

"And Adam was not deceived, but the woman being deceived was in the transgression." I Timothy 2:14 (See Gen. 3:1 and Rom. 6:16).

Commentary: There are two methods that Satan and his devils have always used 1. Lies, and 2. Deception and he does this through temptation, seduction, and promises. Through man's weaknesses of lust for sex, money, and power, and promising these things, man can easily be seduced and deceived into his own world of delusions.

(8:50) In the Holy Scriptures, Satan is described in the following symbolic figures as:

Sower: St. Matthew 13:25
Wolf: St. John 10:12
Lion: I Peter 5:8
Dragon: Revelation 20:2

Bird: St. Matthew 13:4
Man: Ezekial 28:2
Goat: Leviticus 16:25
Trapper: Psalms 91:3

(8:51) In the Holy Scriptures, Satan is called by various names:

Serpent: Rev. 12:9
Destroyer: Psalms 17:4
Wicked One: I John 2:13
Power of Air: Ephesians 2:2
Adversary: I Peter 5:8
Power of Darkness: Colossians 1:13
Devil: Rev. 20:2
Prince of this world: St. John 12:31

Note: Satan's angels, which are now known as or called demons, also have demonic powers in various degrees'.

The Celestial Hierarchies

In intercessions of the angelic host in human affairs are recorded through the Holy writings of all cultures and religions. The Jewish writings of the Old Testament, the Christian writings of the New Testament, The Islam writing of the Koran, and many other writings of various world religions. According to Holy Church, there are other Holy writings, which are not accepted as canon by others. However, those books that were written at the same time or before the New Testament were canonized, and are yet quoted by Christ and the Apostles. To me, these books are just as much canonical as the Gospels themselves, for if the apostles quoted from them, then that means that they accepted them as inspired, and with this, so do I.

The patriarch Enoch lived in the time of Genesis and his life is recorded there "And Enoch walked with God: and he was not; for God took him" Genesis 5:20-24 The book of Enoch are three in numbers and hold within their pages many secrets of the universe. They are listed as non-canonical. Their works are of unknown origin and have been the subject of much theological controversy.

Many of the early Church Fathers and writers frequently made use of these books for references and to learn some of the unknown knowledge (secrets) of the mystical things which the Holy Scriptures do not reveal but is silent. Can the book of Enoch be accepted as divine revelation, inspired works of God? I can only turn to the Holy Scriptures for proof of its foundation into divine revelation.

We know for a fact that Enoch was a real person because it says so in the book of Genesis 5:21-24. We also know that he prophesied. Many scholars place the writings of Enoch 200 years before the birth of Christ, so the books of Enoch existed at the time of the apostles. It is very likely that Christ knew of them, and may have even studied from them as a child, as did John the Baptist and the apostles. The apostle Jude, the cousin of Jesus, knew and accepted them as inspired teachings, for he writes in his letter "And Enoch also, the seventh from Adam, prophesied of these, saying, behold, the Lord cometh with ten thousand of his saints." Jude 14 and 15

It is clear that Jude believed in the existence of Enoch, which is found in Genesis. Many of the early Church fathers, guided by the Holy Spirit, also accepted the books of Enoch as inspired works of God. He used them as canonical as any of the other books of the Bible. Irenaeus and Clement of Alexandria cited and taught from the book of Enoch, without questioning its sacred validity.

Irenaeus accepts the book of Enoch with the same authenticity as the writings of Moses. Tertullian who lived in the beginning of the second century, called the author "The most ancient prophet, Enoch," and of the book of Enoch as the divinely inspired autograph of that immortal patriarch. Because God took him, was preserved by Noah in the ark, and was reproduced by him through the inspiration of the Holy Spirit.

Tertullian states "But as Enoch has spoken in the same scriptures of the Lord, and every scripture suitable for education is divinely inspired." Origen (254 AD) accepts the book of Enoch with the same authority as the Psalms. Let us see some comparison between the book of Enoch and that of the Holy Scriptures.

"It happened after the sons of men had multiplied in those days, that daughter were born of them, elegant and beautiful. And when the angels, the sons of heaven, beheld them, they became enamoured of them, saying to each other, come, let us select for ourselves wives from the progeny of men, and let us beget children." Enoch 7:1 & 2

"And it came to pass, when men began to multiply on the face of the earth, and daughters were born unto them, that the sons of God saw the daughters of men that they were fair; and they took them wives of all which they chose." Genesis 6:1 & 2

Commentary: The Holy Scriptures and the book of Enoch give support to each other on the story of angels taking human women for wives and starting a new breed or race of beings. The sons of heaven are angels, just as the sons of God are angels, for no other creatures at that time lived in heaven but the angelic host. Each book of holy writings is unique in itself, each telling us a little bit more about the universe we live in. The various orders of the Celestial Hierarchies are a well-known fact.

The Celestial Orders

(8:52) Names of the Celestial Orders.

"For by him were all things created, that are in heaven, and that are in earth, visible and invisible, whether they be thrones, or dominions, or principalities, or powers: all things were created by him and for him." Colossians 1:16 (See Ephesians 1:21).

Commentary: St. Paul knew of the Celestial Hierarchy and mentions four of them in his letter to the Colossians, and to the Ephesians 1:21 is mentions "Might" or as other scholars translate it as "Virtues." Between these two verses we are told five names: Thrones, Dominions, Principalities, Powers, and Virtues. Many other scholars and Bible Commentaries understand these five names that St. Paul list to be different levels, powers, or existence of angelic powers or orders. But we need to make something very clear here. St. Paul makes a special statement here that Christ created them all, and he is far above the ranks of these celestial orders.

For many false teachings will, in their understanding, place Christ on the same level of power and authority as the celestial orders. St. Paul corrected this in these two verses, by stating that Christ created them, and we all know that a creature can not be on the same level of that of the Creator. However, the fact remains that St. Paul believed in the existence of these celestial orders. Whether he received this insight from God or he obtained this information from other writers, the point is that he believed in them or he would not have written about them self.

(8:53) Other orders.

"So he drove out the man; and he placed at the east of the garden of Eden Cherubim's…" Genesis 3:24 and "Above it stood the "Seraphims" each on had six wings…" Isaiah 6:2

Commentary: In the book of Genesis we read about God placing a "Cherubim's" at the gate way of the garden of Eden, and around the tree of life in the mist of the garden, so no man may it of its fruit. These Cherubim's are holy angels of God and are one of the celestial orders. In the book of Isaiah we read about the "Seraphims" which are also angels of God, but having six wings. They stand before the glory of God and surround his throne in heaven and give us the divine doxology *"Holy, Holy, Holy, is the Lord of host: the whole earth is full of his glory."* Isaiah 6:3 These Seraphims are holy angels and are the highest of all the celestial orders. Now to complete the list of names, we add the following two names: angels and archangels, and this gives us a total of nine celestial orders.

The Nine Celestial Orders

The celestial hierarchy is based upon the interpretation of the Holy Scriptures and other inspired works and the writings of prominent men and holy men that lived in man's history, such as: St. Ambrose, Pope Gregory Pseudo-Dionysius, St. Jerome, Isidore of Seville, and Gregory the great. The orders of the celestial hierarchy are nine in number; they are Seraphims, Cherubim's, Thrones, Dominion, Powers, Virtues, Principalities, Archangels, and Angels. Each of these orders were established for a reason and purpose, and each have their own powers, authority, duties, function, and divine purpose.

It was the Dionysian system of nine celestial orders, which the apostolic church accepted. The early Protestants disputed it, then later some rejected it. Others in the occult world would write about the celestial orders and try to add to it, to fulfill their personal needs, but the Church and others did not accept these added teachings. Let us review each order and learn as much as possible.

Seraphim: This is the highest of all of the celestial orders. The seraphim surround the throne of God and declare the trisogion "Holy, Holy, Holy." I find it interesting that the angels would say the word "Holy" three times as if they were associating them with the three personage of the Holy Trinity. The book if Isaiah was written long before the doctrine of the trinity came to light. The trisogion are very holy words used by the angels, and it has been used by Holy Church as part of there Divine Liturgy. The seraphim are angels of love and of light, associated with the elements of fire. The trisogion is found in the Holy Scriptures "And one cried unto another, and said, Holy, Holy, Holy, Lord God Almighty, which was, and is, and is to come." Rev. 4:8

The angels of God who stood before God and surround his throne and they are impressed with God's attribute to his holy nature, the perfection of holiness of his character. God sought to impress upon the mind of the prophet Isaiah the concept of his holiness, to keep the divine character before his people so Israel may forget their sins and seek the greater good (reward) of God's holiness. "And the four living beings had each of them six wings about them…and they rest not day and night, saying, Holy, Holy, Holy, Lord God Almighty, which was, and is, and is to come." Rev. 4:8

These are the living beings (angels) that St. John saw. In the King James Version, living beings are labeled as "Beasts" taken from the Greek "Zoa," which means living beings.

Because these angels each have six wings they are of the celestial order of seraphim. In Rev. 4:8 you once again hear the trisogion being repeated. There are four angels of the Seraphims order, which corresponds to the four winds of the world according to the third book of Enoch (see Enoch 18:3 and 26:1-4). "And after these things I saw four angels standing on the Four Corners of the earth, holding the four winds of the earth." These four angels are, according to Rabbinic writings, the same as the *"Hayyoth."* These hayyoth are holy heavenly angels, known as angels of fire (light) they support the throne of glory (God).

According to the book of Enoch the seraphim have four faces and six wings. The Holy Scriptures review of the celestial orders of seraphim can only be found in one place that is the book of Isaiah. Its description of the seraphim angels is more reliable for facts than that of the book of Enoch. However, the book of Enoch sheds a little more light. The word Seraphim is a Hebrew word and it means "Burning Ones" or "Shining Ones." Each of these angels has six wings and used two of their wings to cover their faces in homage and reverence before God.

As Isaiah prayed in the temple court he saw a vision. He saw the temple doors open and in the most holy place "The Holy of Holy" he saw God himself seated upon his throne. The train that Isaiah speaks of is his garments, which shines of God's infinite glory. It is believed these angels to be radiant in nature, giving off intense light that even the other angelic beings can not look upon them.

Cherubim: The cherubim are of an Assyrian and/or Akkadian origin. In the Akkadian tongue it means "one who prays" or "one who intercedes." In the ancient artwork of the Assyrians, a cherubim was pictured as a huge winged creature. According to Hebrew understanding the name Cherubim interpreted as "fullness of knowledge." They posses the knowledge of God and hold the fullness of the science of heaven.

In the Canaanites lore there cherubim were thought of as angels. According to the book of Ezekiel in chapter 10:20, 21 they are creatures of heaven having four wings "“his is the living creatures that I saw under the God of Israel by the river of Chebar; and I knew that they were the Cherubim’s. Every one had four faces apiece, and every one four wings…” After the fall of man from the state of grace, the tree of life was protected by a cherubim angel with a flaming sword. They also guarded the entrance of the Garden of Eden (Gen. 3:23, 24). These winged creatures symbolized God’s highest and chief sovereignty, goodness, and authority.

Cherubim were the angels of the Ark of the Covenant, placed right above the mercy seat. The cherubim are listed second in rank of the celestial hierarchy and are the guardians of the fixed stars. They are the angels of light who excel in knowledge and keep the records of the celestial orders.

Thrones: The celestial order of thrones rank third of the nine orders of the hierarchy. There is not much information about this order. The apostle Paul mentioned it in Colossians 1:16 about thrones and three other orders. He named them because he knew of them, and believed in them, or he would not have mentioned them. They are also known as “Ophanim” that carry out God’s judgments. They are angels of peace and stress humility in their ministry for the Lord.

Dominions: This is the fourth order in the rank of the celestial hierarchy. Here they regulate angel’s duties and are forever loyal to God. It is through this order that the power of God manifest them selves. (See Ephesians 1:20, 21 and Enoch 20:1 and Levi 1:25). They are overseers of the other angels receiving their instructions from the Seraphim and Cherubim. Only on various occasions do they reveal themselves to mortals.

Virtues: This is the fifth order of the celestial hierarchy. The main duty of this angelic order is to work miracles on earth. They are the chief angels that bestow the blessing or gift of grace. It is believed by some that these angels are the same that Jesus talks about in the Gospel of St. Matthew 18:10. This class of angelic beings are also called the "Blessing Angels." For they are always bestowing there blessing upon the material world. They govern the movement of the celestial bodies in our universe and influence or control the weather here on earth.

Powers: It was the Greek Septuagint which first used the word powers to associate with the angelic order. The main duty of this order is to stop any effort of the demons that would overthrow the world. According to the writings of Pope Gregory, it was his view that the celestial order of powers presides over demons. The powers have a great responsibility in their duties for the Lord, for they stand between dimensions as guardians, forever guarding the celestial doors or pathways between two realms and between heaven and earth. They are the elite guard that protects against demonic attacks. The powers are the major line of defense.

Principalities: This order is the protector of religion and watchers over the leaders of people. Their influence at times helps them to make right decisions. This order was talked and written about as far back as the second century BC when St. Ignatius Martyr (d.107), touching on the ranks of angels in the "Epistle to the Trallians," spoke of the hierarchy of principalities. They are the guardians of our world and protectors of towns and cities. They work with the invisible things of our world. They are the protectors of religious leaders.

Archangels: These are the angels of higher rank, above the grade of angels and man. In the Old Testament they are referred to be of a higher order, thus becoming the eight rank of the celestial orders. They are also the seven angels who stand before the throne of God "And I saw the seven angels who stood before God; and to them were given seven trumpets." Rev. 8:2

Angels: A created being, having supernatural powers and at times act as an intermediate between God and man. They are talked and written about by almost every religion on earth, they at times are referred to as spirits or angels. They are in the Holy Scriptures and all other non-canonical books. They are highly brilliant creatures, having wings.

The Ninth Order of Divinity

"The Creation of Man"

I John Paul, a Servant of Christ Jesus, by the Grace of God, write this commentary on the *creation of man.* May my blessings be upon you and peace from God our Father and from our Lord Jesus of Nazareth called the Christ. There are times when we become so involved in our daily lives and problems, we seldom take the time to observe the events and changes around us. It is at this time that even the simplest of things may elude our attention. Man throughout the countless centuries has always sought to understand and study his own spiritual nature. I say spiritual because we are created in the likeness and image of our Creator. We were given his divine spirit that animates life, thereby making us a spiritual creature. We think and reason, we posses the ability of creative thought and imagination, and we have the freedom to chose. All these attribute are given to our Creator and we in his likeness also posses these same traits.

However, we are taught that man is a helpless creature, unable to do for himself, without the blessing or intervention of God. I personally do not accept such doctrine and beliefs. I believe that man is unable to obtain salvation by himself without God's intervention, for only by God's grace, through faith in Christ Jesus, are we saved. I understand that God creates all things, and everything we have in our life comes from God. However, God has given to man the ability and the will, through his intelligence and imagination, to care for himself and to carve, shape, and make his own destiny, which is part of his freedom of choice. Allow me to give you an example, God has created the seed to grow food, but it will grow only if man first plant the seed into the ground. Only through a joined effort between God and man will the seed grow. Man plants the seed and God works the miracle of life that makes the seed grow. Yes, God could have spoken the word and food would appear, but then there would be no need for a seed. God created the seed for man to use and sustain him self, to learn and know the miracle of life that comes from God.

At the time of creation in regards to our spiritual nature, and our state of grace we were deemed lower than the angels, after the fall, but still a babe in the truth and knowledge of our existence. At the appointed time our Creator posed a test of obedience upon man. Sin (evil) entered into our world through Satan. For Satan influence Eve and through his power of temptation caused her to disobey God. Adam out of love for Eve and not for God followed his wife into sin and also disobeyed God. So our first parents failed the test of obedience in the Garden of Eden, their spiritual nature and his state of grace also fell and became less than that of the angels, yet remained higher than that of the animal kingdom.

The Nature of Man

Birth is the beginning of all life, physical, spiritual, and organic, here on earth, and we very seldom take a close look at the process behind it. I am not talking about the physical aspect of birth, but of the spiritual aspect. The Holy Scriptures provides for us the understanding and knowledge of our creation. Adam, according to the Bible, was the first man ever created.

(9:1) Created Man.

"And the Lord God formed man of the dust of the ground, and breathed into his nostrils the breath of life; and man became a living soul." Genesis 2:7

Commentary: The Holy Scriptures gives us a good detailed account of Adam's creation, and it also allows us to view God's workshop, the universe. We can witness the divine works of his hands, performing the mystical workings of creation. Close your eyes and use your own divine gift of imagination and watch God molding and fashioning into a form and physical body of Adam, according to the design of His divine plan.

Man's physical structure is composed of the same material and elements derived from the earth, and science has confirmed this, as the body decomposition after death bears witness. The four major elements from which all of creation is derived are Oxygen, Carbon, Hydrogen, and Nitrogen. These four arranged in proper order make up the human body.

After Adam's body was formed, God gave him a very special gift; he gave to Adam a part of his own being. The breath of life or spiritual life principles entered into the lifeless body of Adam. It sparked into existence a divine life, possessing a part of the Creator's own spirit. The spiritual aspect behind the creation of man is the breath of life, which God gave to man, freely, by breathing into man's physical body his very own life-giving spirit. It is through this union that we are one with God in spirit. Through this union we are able to move, breathe, and have our being.

(9:2) St. Paul write about man's creation.

"For in him we live, and move, and have our being; as certain also of your own poets have said, for we are also his offspring." Acts 17:28

Commentary: Paul is expressing his thoughts that all of our activities; physical, mental, and spiritual, are derived from God, because by him we have our life experience and through him we have our total existence. Our first parents (Adam & Eve) as like all of us are made up of two vital elements 1. *Physical Body:* made from the same elements found in the earth, 2. *Spiritual Essence:* an energy or life force, which gives all living things life.

It is time for us to understand in Biblical Research, the meaning of the human soul. In the King James Version of Genesis 2:7 it states, *"And man became a living soul."* In other modern translations, the word "Being" or "Person" is used instead of the word "soul." The word soul is a name that describes the existence of the human consciousness.

The creation of a human being is the joining of the two vital elements of nature, the physical body and a Spiritual essence. At the moment of conception these two elements are integrated. We have the creation of man's Conscious existence, the human soul. At this time man began to express creative thought, and exercise the power of imagination. My comments here are not to be taken for anything that might describe the possible existence of a conscious entity outside the human body. When we take two parts of hydrogen and join it with one part oxygen, we have the creation known as "water." The word water is only a name that describes the joining of two elements, in this example its hydrogen and oxygen.

You have a light bulb, which in metaphor terms, can be used to represent the human body, then you have electricity, which in the same metaphor manner can be attribute to the spirit of God. When electricity enters the light bulb it lights up, when the spirit of God enters the human body the human mind lights up, and God has created life, a being, a person, a conscious soul, with the ability of free choice and the ability of creative thought.

When the electricity is turned off, the light stops shinning, it ceases to exist. Whenever the body becomes damaged beyond repair and the spirit leaves the body, the person dies. And the physical life within ceases. However, the conscious soul, according to some Christian theology believe, that the conscious soul lives on, but in an unconscious state, or exists in a state of sleep, until the second coming of Christ. The Roman Catholic, Orthodox Catholic, Old Catholic, Anglican Catholic believe that the conscious soul lives on and goes to heaven or hell at the time of death. Yet, other Christian churches are divided between these two theological teachings.

(9:3) God creates woman.

"And the Lord God said, it is not good that the man should be alone; I will make him an help meet for him…" Gen. 2:18. *"And the Lord God caused a deep sleep to fall upon Adam, and he slept: and he took one of his ribs, and closed up the flesh instead thereof; And the rib, which the Lord God had taken from man, made he a woman, and brought her unto the man."* Gen. 2:21,21.

Commentary: At that this time when Adam met Eve, we understand that this was an arranged marriage, God being the matchmaker. We must remember that Adam and Eve did not have the opportunity to experience the process of growing up, but were created as adults. Eve was created for Adam, as his equal and as a mate. Establishing a relationship of love and friendship, each to offer companionship to one another. To multiply and populate the earth.

Adam and Eve were created as illumines beings, made by God, wrapped in a robe of light. It was not until they fell from God's grace that their body became stained with the sin of disobedient and the robe of light left them. They saw themselves naked and covered themselves with leaves, because they were ashamed and embarrass and hid from the face of God (Gen. 3:9-10).

Man as a illumines being created by the hand of God and wrapped in his glory, stood before the face of God, perfect in God's image, walked with him in the Garden of Eden.

All of man, no matter what race, color, creed, culture, or religion, all have the same forefather, the same beginning and history, the same genetic make-up in Adam, including the stain of original sin.

Theological Concept of Unconscious Sleep

It seems very simple to understand once you have studied the Scriptures from all sources and use your common sense. When the time comes for us to depart this world, the two vital elements of life shall return unto the source from which it came.

(9:4) At the time of death.

"Then shall the dust return to the earth as it was: and the spirit shall return unto God who gave it." Ecclesiastes 12:7

Commentary: Each vital elements return to its proper place. The body decays and returns to the earth from where it came, and the spirit shall return unto God who first gave it. But what happens to our soul? The teachings of some Protestant churches believe that at the time of death, the conscious mind (soul) continues to live. At the time of death our conscious soul enters into an unconscious state of existence according to how they interpret the Holy Scriptures. This is called the state of sleep concept. All levels of consciousness still exist; the subconscious and the conscious mind become dormant and enter a state of sleep. We are cut off from all life, events, and activities of the physical known world. We lie dormant for a little while, preserved by God and held unto the day of resurrection. Then our conscious soul is returned into a new body, fashioned after the likeness of Jesus body, and at the time of the resurrection, we receive immortality. Remember that in a state of sleep it is taught that we have no recollection of time. A thousand years may pass, but to the person who lies dead, only a second of time has passed, then our eyes will be opened and we become part of the day of resurrection.

To the Roman Catholics, Orthodox Catholic, Old Catholics, and many Protestant Churches believe that at death, our soul goes to heaven, in a conscious state and we receive our reward. Whether our body is in a spiritual existence or in a real physical existence is left up to the individual interpretation of his and her personal theology and understanding. The Holy Scriptures can be taken from a literal interpretation or from a symbolic or figurative interpretation. Depending on which perspective you are viewing will determine what theological concept is being presented. Research, study and prayer must be done in order to understand the divine mystery that God has revealed to us.

(9:5) The Holy Scriptures on the resurrection day.

"For the Lord himself shall descend from heaven with a shout, with the voice of the archangel, and with the trump of God: and the dead in Christ shall rise first: then we which are alive and remain shall be caught up together with them in the clouds, to meet the Lord in the air: and so shall we ever be with the Lord." I Thessalonians 4:16, 17

Commentary: At the time of the resurrection, Christ shall may come from the east, or his coming may be swift as lighting *"For as the lightning cometh out of the east, and shineth even unto the west; so shall also the coming of the Son of man be."* St. Matthew 24:27, and we shall all hear the voice of the archangel (proclaim his coming), and the trump of God will sound. When this happens, those people who entered death with the faith of Christ, will be awaken on resurrection day, and the angels of God will gather them up, and will be taken up, into the earth's atmosphere to meet our Lord Jesus Christ in the air. Christ at his coming will never touch his foot upon the earth. Those people who are alive and remain at the second coming, and have the faith of Christ, will also be gather by the angels of the Lord, and all will then be taken to Paradise where our Almighty Father is, and there shall we be ever with the Lord.

(9:6) Events on resurrection day?

"Behold, I show you a mystery; we shall not all sleep, but we shall all be changed. In a moment, in the twinkling of an eye, at the last trump: for the trumpet shall sound, and the dead shall be raised incorruptible, and we shall be changed…" I Cor. 15:51-53

Commentary: In Christian theology, this is the free gift of God, the gift of eternal life. This gift is received at the time of the resurrection only, except when there is an intervention of God. Man has always wondered what it is like after death. Let us review the teaching of the Holy Scriptures on the subject of death, not mans doctrine, but God instruction.

The Holy Scriptures frequently refers to death as a state of sleep. Reading the Holy Scriptures from a literal point of view, the following verses will give us the concept that death is a state of sleep. (I Kings 2:10 and 11:43 and 14:20 and 15:8 and II Chronicles 21:1, and 26:3)

Job 7:21: *"for now shall I sleep in the dust"* see 14:10-12

Psalms 13:3: *"…lighten mine eyes, lest I sleep the sleep of death"*

Jeremiah 51:39: *"and sleep a perpetual sleep"*

Daniel 12:2: *"and many of them that sleep in the dust of the earth shall awake"*

St. Matthew 9:24: *"He said unto them, give place: for the maid is not dead, but sleepeth…"* See also St. Mark 5:39 and St. John 11:11-14

II Peter 3:4: *"And saying, where is the promise of his coming? For since the father fell asleep, all things continue as they were from the beginning of creation."*

I Cor. 15:51: *"we shall not all sleep"*

Sleep according to the Holy Scriptures, is a fitting symbol or explanation of death, an unconscious state of existence, that is another concept. So when you go to sleep tonight you will know what it is like to experience death. Having no knowledge of the world and events around you.

Death! The Unconscious Sleep

(9:7) Unconsciousness sleep.

"The dead know not anything" Ecclesiastes 9:5

Commentary: It is clearly stated that people to have died know not anything, they have no knowledge of the things that are going on around them, no conscious thoughts, or understanding of anything under the sun. Are we to take this verse literally? Does this support the theological concept of death as an unconscious state of existence? Or can it be that when we are taken to heaven we enter into another realm of existence that cuts us off from the physical world we just left behind, and are unable to know anything that is going on in this world with our family, friends, and world events?

(9:8) Our thoughts at the time of death.

"In that very day his thoughts persih" Psalms 146:4

Commentary: In the very second of our death, our ability to think, to exercise our imagination, or use our ability of creative thought stops. It is interesting to note that if we where to go straight to heaven at our time of death, and it is literally true that our thoughts perish at the very moment of death, then we would become mindless beings walking around in heaven. To receive our reward at the time of our death removes the need for a judgement day or a day of resurrection, doesn't it? The Apostle Paul believed and taught of a real physical resurrection as our reward, obtained at the

Second Coming of Christ, not at our death. Does this verse support the theological concept of death being a state of unconscious sleep? Our thoughts here on earth may perish for it can no longer function within our decaying body at the time of our death. This does not mean that our conscious soul cannot be translated into heaven in a heavenly body and perceive heavenly thoughts, like those of the angels. Then later at the appointed time, at the second coming, on resurrection day once again be given "immortality," but physical body such as the one's Adam and Eve had before their fall, Fashioned after the likeness of the risen Christ.

(9:9) All daily activities stop.

"Whatsoever thy hand findeth to do, do it with thy might; for there is no work, nor device, nor knowledge, nor wisdom, in the grave, whither thou goest" Ecclesiastes 9:10

Commentary: This is why it is important not to worry about little things that go on in this world, but that we live our life to the fullest measure, and not to let any minor things annoy us. Don't be troubled by unimportant things. Don't trouble your pondering on the things you have no control over, find peace and joy in the things that you are doing now, today. Anything that you can find joy in doing in this world, do it with great love, and do the best you can. Once you enter the grave, all activities stop, because there is no device, knowledge, wisdom, or works in the grave, that is very much apart of this world.

(9:10) All our emotions stop.

"Also their love, and their hatred and their envy is now perished: neither have they any more a portion for ever in anything that is done under the Sun." Ecclesiastes 9:6

Commentary: All emotions are gone. The dead cannot experience love, hatred, envy, nor have anything to do under the Sun. Strong emotions are part of our being part of our nature, in death they serve no function. Another point of interest to take note of, the Holy Scriptures says that when we die our emotions all perish. For what reason or purpose then does a ghost or entity have for returning to earth from the grave, if this is possible, if they have no love, envy, hatred, or any kind of emotion then they have no reason. Then who are these ghost or spirits that we see and hear, but another trick that Satan and his demons play to get people to believe that we have a immortal soul *"And the serpent said unto the woman, ye shall not surely die."* Genesis 3:4 Satan was telling his lies to Eve, and he still tells them to us today.

It is true, once we experience our physical death here on earth all of our emotions perish, because our human emotions are tied to our physical existence through the chemical resections that took part in our physical bodies. Remember what the Apostle Paul said, upon our salvation in Jesus Christ? All things will become new again and that is true for our body, mind, spirit, and emotions. Be careful not to interpret every verse in a literal sense. We will have emotions in heaven as new creatures.

(9:11) The human, a temple of God.

"Know ye not that ye are the temple of God, and that the spirit of God dwelleth in you." I Cor. 3:16

Commentary: The spirit of God lives within each of us and it gives us life. Our bodies constitute a spiritual building or temple for the indwelling spirit of God. We should not defile this temple through improper diet and living habits. We should not give up our spiritual practices of humility, daily prayer, going to church every worship day, and studying the Holy Scriptures.

Man's Stewardship

Man was given dominion over the earth. God appointed man as the caretaker of all life on the earth. As steward over all life on the earth, man was given responsibility, and with responsibility, there must be some day of reckoning, an accounting of his actions. God is the Creator and owner of all life, and his steward (man) will be held responsible for all that was placed under his care. At the appointed time, the steward will be called upon to make personal account of what he did with God" creation. So we should think twice before we choice to pollute our environment, or before we choice to abuse our Forest, and as caretaker when we mistreat any kind of pet or animal. God's birds, animals, insects, and all creeping thinks are under our care.

(9:12) Man's responsibility.

"And God said, let us make man in our image, after our likeness: and let them have dominion over the fish of the sea, and over the fowl of the air, and over the cattle, and over all the earth, and over every creeping thing that creepeth upon the earth. " Gen. 1:26

Commentary: We were given the great honor of bearing God's image and likeness, both as an outward sign and as a spiritual inward nature. Characterizing God's pure, just, and righteous nature, holding within our creation the endowed ability of free will, imagination, and a self-conscious personality.

Our relationship to all other life on earth is one of rulership. God uses the plural word "them" in Gen. 1:26 to indicate that it is his intention to create more than one person as care-taker of his creation. God says "Let us make man" can imply that God is consulting the trinity of the Godhead or consulting the other divine beings (immortal beings, possessing eternal life) other than the trinity on the creation of man. Who was God talking to? However, it may have been the custom of kings, priests, and scribes to speak in a plural content as a form of majesty. It was the custom of the Persians to practice this tradition. Another example is the how the Pope of Rome talks; who always uses the word "We" as a plural statement when addressing cardinals, bishops, and other clergy, referring to God and himself whom is speaking.

(9:13) Man's dominion over all living things

"Thou madest him (man) to have dominion over the works of thy hands; thou hast put all things under his feet: all sheep and oxen, yea, and the beasts of the fields: The fowl of the air, and the fish of the sea, and whatsoever passeth through the path of the seas." Ps. 8:6-8

Commentary: Many scholars or commentary writers may deny man's dominion over the wild beasts of the earth, yet in Psalms 8: 6-8 man's dominion is repeated and the beasts of the fields are included. The key phrase in this verse is *"Thou hast put all things under his feet,"* including the wild beasts of the field. It is only my opinion but the beasts of the fields can refer to the dinosaurs as the beasts, which died out later, before the appearance of Moses, whom God dictated the events of creation and Moses recorded what the Lord told him.

Dinosaurs could have become instinct because of a worldwide event such as the great flood of Noah's time. A worldwide flood could have brought on an ice age over the northern part of the earth. A large mass of water could have shifted the earth on its axis causing an ice age. An ice age does not have to encompass an entire planet, but can effect only various parts of the planet. However, according to how the earth rotation on its axis was effected will determine the type of ice age. As the water found various cracks in the earth and began to recessed filling valleys and creating lakes and oceans. The earth rotation was again shifted on its axis centuries later and this shift returned the earth to its original position, which we see it today, slowly ending the ice age.

(9:14) God ownership.

"The earth is the Lord's, and the fullness thereof; the world, and they that dwell therein." Ps.24: 1

Commentary: In Psalms the author claims God's right of ownership over the earth, and all of the inhabitants therein. The management of God's creation was given to man, this is why God put man in the midst of the Garden, to inhabit it, and to keep it (Gen. 2:15), (read also Ps. 115:16).

(9:15) Man's fall.

"So he drove out the man; and he placed at the east of the Garden of Eden Cherubins, and a flaming sword which turned every way, to keep the way of the tree of life." Gen. 3:24

Commentary: Since man failed his test of obedience God decreed that man shall labor and earn his living. This must have been a very sad decision God made as a father, teaching his children the wrong they did, and setting fort their punishment. As Adam and Eve went forth into the world they would labor hard for the food, for their existences. They will face hardship, weeds, insects, and wild beasts.

The fall of Man

(9:16) What is Sin?

"Whatsoever committeth sin transgresseth also the law: for sin is the transgression of the law." I John 3:4

Commentary: From the Greek *"hamartia"* which means *"a wrong deed," "a sin."* From the *"hamartano"* to do wrong. John clearly explains sin as disobedient to the divine laws and moral laws of God. Paul takes it a step forward, stating that result of sin can be passed on to the next generation. This is the stain of original sin (the disobedience of Adam and Eve) which is passed on to every generation. As Paul writes *"Wherefore, as by one man sin entered into the world, and death by sin; and so death passed upon all men, for that all have sinned."* Rom. 5:12

The law of God is an image of his divine character, and having created us he has decreed that if we love him we will submit ourselves to his will and become obedient to his law. All who transgress and that break the law or go beyond the extent of the law or to over ride the law or to go against the law, just to justify his or her actions commith a sin.

(9:17) The result of sin.

"For the wage of sin is death; but the gift of God is eternal life through Jesus Christ our Lord." Rom. 6:23

Commentary: The wage of sin is death there is no other way of translating or interpreting this verse. Those who knowingly love and practice sin shall receive their just reward of death. However, those who accept Jesus Christ as their Lord and Saviour will prove their faith by their willingness to follow God's teachings and become obedient to God's laws, this in turn will insure them of their salvation under grace. Do you think the man who professes his faith in Jesus Christ as his Saviour, and goes on sinning, do you think he is saved? Jesus said it *"Many will say to me in that day, Lord, Lord, have we not prophesied in thy name? And in thy name have cast out devils? And in thy name done many wonderful works? And then will I profess unto them, I never knew you: depart from me, ye that work iniquity."* Matt. 7:22-24

In the Jewish tradition they celebrate the feast of "Passover" when the angel of death passed over of the house of Israel in the time of Moses, thereby saving the Jewish race. The divine gift of grace is the Christian Passover and all found in the book of life is passed over from the stain of original sin, and all who's name is written in the book of life are untouched and thereby saved unto eternal life. The state of grace is a free gift from God. All who are saved are under the state of grace. Is your name written in the book of life?

(9:18) The altering of all creation.

"…Cursed is the ground for thy sake; in sorrow shalt thou eat of it all the days of thy life; thorns also and thistles shall it bring forth to thee; and thou shalt eat the herb of the field." Gen. 3: 17, 18

Commentary: For our good, God cursed the ground and the earth (Mother Nature) and the earth turned against man. In sorrow and suffering, with hard labor and in sweat shall we ever more bring forth food from the earth until the day of judgement. It is interesting to note that God did not curse Adam or Eve but he cursed the ground. This shows that God loved Adam and Eve. It was also told to Adam and Eve that she, in sorrow and pain, will bring forth life in the time of childbearing. Another point of interest is that God changes man diet, so that the quantity and quality of fruits, vegetables, herbs, grains, nuts, beans and seeds shall become our stable source of food.

Man's Redemption

(9:19) The Messiah must suffer.

"But he was wounded for our transgressions, he was bruised for our iniquities: the chastisement of our peace was upon him; and with his stripes we are healed." Isa. 53:5

Commentary: The Messiah shall suffer for us a great chastisement for payment of our sins, and to re-establish a relationship between God and man, he shall become that bridge of peace. Because of the law that was written by God, that condemned us, only a God with equal authority can make things right with the law. Out of great love God chose to suffer for us and be chastised. The Christian faith is the only religion on earth that can say "my God came down and died for my sins and saved me." For man through his weakness is unable to save him self, having no authority of himself equal unto the law to make things right.

(9:20) The reason for the Messiah coming.

"And ye know that he was manifested to take away our sins; and in him is no sin." I John 3:5

Commentary: The apostle John told his reader of the plan of God salvation. This is why he states "And ye know" of the Messiah purpose was to make known, to reveal God's plan, of the Messiah incarnation, sinless life, and of his great suffering he must pay to make things right between God and man. To establish the state of grace from which all is protected from the law, in matters of original sin.

However, with out the law, we would not know sin, yet sin is an influencing, dominating, and controlling force, which acts upon our weakness. Jesus victory over the power of sin was declared upon the cross, as he himself as God, who was sinless, paid the ultimate price to gain victory over the power of sin. In doing this he established our salvation and declared his ultimate love for us.

(9:21) St. Paul writing about God and sin?

"For the wage of sin is death; but the gift of God is eternal life through Jesus Christ our Lord." Rom. 6:23

Commentary: Do not allow yourself the pleasure of entertaining sinful thoughts, less you fall under its power of influence and become a sinner. For the rewards of sin is death. Not just a physical death that can later be resurrected, but a spiritual death, both body and soul together joined in death is a complete death that is eternal.

All sin starts in the mind where, if allowed to fester and grow, will finally be acted out and committed.

Sin rewards those people who love and practice sin and receive exactly what they have earned. We find in the writings of Ezekiel *"The soul that sinneth, it shall die."* Eze. 18:4 Death is the opposite of eternal life, and we are given the choice as to what kind of life we wish to live. What is remarkable is that God's gift of eternal life is free, and all he asks from us is to accept his teachings, and obey his laws. The laws of God was established for our good, for our benefit and understanding (I John 5:11).

When we receive eternal life it will be in a world where there is no pain or sickness. You will never grow old. There will be no sin, nor fear, or anger and hatred, or any bad emotions. A world where all animals are as gentle pets and the lion will lie down with the lamb and a child will lead them (Isa. 11: 6-9). Harmony shall be established among all the creatures of the world.

Biblical References

I. Theological:

1. The Bible, written by Josh McDowell and Don Stewart, Published by Here's Life Publishing, Inc., San Bernardino, California, 1979

2. Early Christian Doctrines, written by J.N.D. Kelly, published by Harper & Row, Publishers, New York, 1978

3. Christian Apologetics, written by Norman L. Geisler, Published by Prince Press, 2002

4. Bible Reading for the Home, put together by the Seventh - day Adventist Church, Published by Review and Herald Publishing, Washington, D.C. 1979

5. Practical Christian Theology, written by Floyd H. Barackman, Published by Fleming H. Revell company, Old Tappan, New Jersey, 1984

6. The Book of Jewish Knowledge by Nathan Ausubel, Published by Crown Publishers, Inc., New York, 1964

II. Bible Commentary:

7. Seventh-day Adventist Bible Commentary, Published by Review and Herald Publishing Association, Washington, D.C. 1980

8. The Interpreter's Bible, Published by Abingdon Press, Nashville Ten. 1989

III. Biblical Concordances & Dictionary:

9. Strong's Exhaustive Concordance of the Bible, by James Strong, S.T.D., LL.D Published by Macdonald publishing company, Mclean, Virginia,

10. Strong's Concordance of the bible, by James Strong, S.T.D.,LL.D. Published by Thomas Nelson Publishers, Nashville, 1980

11. Expository Dictionary of Bible Words, by Lawrence O. Richards, Published by Regency Reference Library, Zondervan Publishing House, Grand Rapids, Michigan, 1985

12. Young's Bible Dictionary, by G. Douglas Young, Ph.D., Published by Tyndale House Publishers, Inc. Wheaton, Illinois, 1984

13. Today's Dictionary of the Bible, compiled by T. A. Bryant, Published by Bethany House Publishers, Minneapolis, Minnesota, 1982

14. Catholic Encyclopedia, by New Advent, Kevin Knight, 2007

15. Catholic Encyclopedia, by Broderick, Robert C., Our Sunday Visitor, Inc. 1976

IV. Others

The Celestial Hierarchy by Dionysius Areopagiticus

Appendix-A

Other Works

I. Bible Study Courses

1. The Holy Trinity
2. Eternal Message

II. Other Book printed

1. A Primer on Biblical Studies

III. Up Coming Books

2. The Biblical Study of the Pentateuch
3. Catholic Talmud "Volume two" "The Anointed"

VI. Recommend Seminary

I recommend "Agape" Seminary as a fine school to study for the priesthood or to earn a religious degree at a very fair tuition. The school is licensed by the state of Florida.

Agape Seminary
P. O Box 7078
Clearwater, Fl. 33758

I have set aside my Church ministry, devoting myself to study, research and teaching. I am looking for a teaching position to teach Biblical Studies or Biblical Theology with some University, College or Seminary. I am open to any offers.

Dr. John Paul Hozvicka D.D.
15959 Ashland Drive
Brook Park, Ohio 44142
USA

Appendix-B

"Apostolic Succession"

It has been ten years now since I laid down my duty and practice as a priest and consecrated bishop. But have not given up my ministry for my Lord and Savior Jesus of Nazareth called the Christ; but have dedicated my self to the academic study, research and teaching of the Holy Scriptures.

I present my apostolic succession here because I am blessed to have received it and my lineage can be traced back to St. Peter, then to Jesus Christ, and finally to God. At times I can feel the power of the Holy Spirit flowing through me as I write my thoughts and share the Lords blessings with others. I guest it's the Roman Catholic in me.

The Most Rev. John Paul Hozvicka D.D., SCJ
July 14, 1991

The Most Rev Norman R. Parr D.D.
Oct. 23, 1979

The Most Rev. Grant Timothy Billet
Dec. 25, 1950

The most Rev. Earl Anglin James
June 17, 1945

The Most Rev. Carmel Henry Carfora
Oct. 4, 1916

The Most Rev. De Landas Berghes
June 29, 1913

The Most Rev. Arnold Harris Mathew
April 28, 1908

Old Catholic Church

Bishop Gerardus Gul, May 11, 1892
Bishop Gaspard Johannes Rinkel, August 11, 1873
Bishop Herman Heykamp, 1853
Bishop Johannes Van Santen, Nov. 3, 1825
Bishop Johannes Bon, April 25, 1819
Bishop Willibrord Van OS, April 24, 1814
Bishop Gisbert De Jong, Nov. 7, 1805
Bishop Johannes Jacobus Van Rhijn, July 5, 1797
Bishop Adrian Broekman, 1778
Bishop Walter Van Nieuwenhuisen, Feb. 7, 1768
Bishop Johannes Van Stiphout, 1745
Bishop Petrus Johannes Meindaerts, Oct18, 1739
Bishop Dominique Marie Varlet, Feb 19, 1719
Bishop De Matignon, 1693
Bishop Jacques Benigne Bossuet, 1670
Bishop Charles Maurice Letellier, 1667

Note: The Old Catholic Church separated its self from the Roman Catholic Church in 1667. However, the apostolic succession is pure and true, unbroken and alive.

Roman Catholic

Cardinal Antonio Barberini, 1657
Nephew of Pope Urban VIII

Pope Alexander VII, April 7, 1655

Index

The First Order of Divinity

The Third Order of Divinity

The Fourth Order of Divinity

I. The Creator and His Creation

II. The Character and Attribute to God

III. The Love of God

The Fifth Order of Divinity

I. Fifteen Facts about Jesus

II. The Deity of Christ

The Sixth Order of Divinity

I. The Holy Spirit

13. How does Jesus spiritually enter believers? (6:13)-117

II. Fruits of the Spirit

1. What is the fruits of the spirit? (6:14)-117
2. What are the works of the flesh (6:15)-117
3. How may the works of the flesh be avoided? (6:16)-118
4. What does the Holy Spirit have to do with love? (6:17)-118
5. What does the heavenly kingdom consist of? (6:19)-119
6. How does God regard those Christian who practice a meek and quiet spirit? (6:19)-119
7. What is said about all the virtues of the fruit of the Holy Spirit? (6:20)-119
8. To what unity are Christian exhorted? (6:21)-120

III. Gifts of the Holy Spirit

1. What should we, as Christian, be concerned about? (6:22)-120
2. When Christ went up to heaven, what did he give to men? (6:23)-121
3. What were the gifts Christ gave? (6"24)-121
4. What is obtained as a result of the uses of these gifts? (6:25)-121
4. What is the manifestation of the one spirit? (6:26)-122
   A.) Word of wisdom-122
   B.) Word of knowledge-122
   C.) Faith-123
   D.) Gift of healing-123
   E.) Gift of prophecy-123
   F.) Discerning Spirits-124
   G.) Speaking in tongues-124

The Eight Order of Divinity

III. Angelic Host

IV. Dark Ministry of Evil Angels

VI. The Origin of Evil

1. With whom did sin originate? (8:38)-150
2. Who committed first murder? (8:39)-150
3. What relationship is there between Satan and the act of lying? (8:40)-151
4. Was Satan created sinful? (8:41)-151
5. What led Satan to sin? (8:42)-151
   a.) Corruption-151
   b.) Fall-151
   c.) Rebellion-151
   d.) Cast into Hell-151

VII. Satanic Powers

1. Power of temptation (8:43)-152
2. Power of Miracles (8:44)-152
3. Power of Possess (8:45)-153
4. Power to take on animal form (8:46)-153
5. Power of transformation (8:47)-153
6. With whom does Satan occupy his time (8:48)-154
7. Satan's methods of Evil (8:49)-154
8. In the Holy Scriptures, Satan is described in the following symbolic figures as. (8:50)-154
9. In the Holy Scriptures, Satan is called by various names (8:41)-155

VIII. The Celestial Orders

Enoch-157
Book of Jude-157
Irenawus-157
Tertullian-157

1. What are the names of the Celestial Orders? (8:52)-158
2. Does the Bible name any other Orders? (8:53)-158

3. In death (sleep), does it bring an end to all the days activities? (9:9)-174
4. In death (sleep), are all motions rendered inactive? (9:10)-174
5. Is our body a temple, built by God? (9:11)-175

IV. Man's Stewardship

1. At the time of man's creation, what responsibility was given to man? (9:12)-176
2. Did man have dominion over the beasts (wild animals) of the fields? (9:13)-177
3. Who has real ownership over the earth and all that live on it? (9:14)-178
4. When man failed as caretaker, what did God do? (9:15)-178

V. The Fall of Man

1. What is Sin? (9:16)-178
2. What is the result of sin? (9:17)-179
3. What happen to all of creation because of man's sin? (9:18)-179

VI. Man's Redemption

1. What does the prophet Isaiah say about the suffering the messiah will endure for our sins? (9:19)-180
2. For what purpose did the Messiah come to earth? (9:20)-181
3. What does Paul write about God and Sin? (9:21)-181

www.ingramcontent.com/pod-product-compliance
Ingram Content Group UK Ltd.
Pitfield, Milton Keynes, MK11 3LW, UK
UKHW020143250726
13967UKWH00002B/826

9 781425 171629